THE

FAILURE OF POLITICAL EXTREMISM

IN

INTER-WAR BRITAIN

Edited by Andrew Thorpe

EXETER STUDIES IN HISTORY No. 21

EXETER STUDIES IN HISTORY

General Editor: Colin Jones, BA DPhil FRHistS

Editorial Committee

J. Barry, MA DPhil

D. C. Braund, MA PhD

M. Duffy, MA DPhil FRHistS

R. A. Higham, BA PhD

M. D. D. Newitt, BA PhD FRHistS

Printed in Great Britain by BPCC Wheatons Ltd, Exeter

Contents

Acknowledgements

The papers in this volume were originally presented at a one-day conference held at the University of Exeter on 12 May 1988. I would like to thank all those visiting academics, colleagues and students who attended and participated in the conference, and especially the contributors who have made my job as editor such an easy and enjoyable one. The Department of History and Archæology generously helped with the conference expenses. I would also like to acknowledge the permission of the various holders for permission to quote from documents for which they hold the copyright: Unwin Hyman for *The British System of Government* by A.H. Birch; Routledge for *The Politics of Democratic Socialism* by E.F.M. Durbin. Finally my thanks go to my colleagues Dr Colin Jones, general editor of the series, for all his assistance and encouragement, and Dr Michael Duffy, who proof-read with great efficiency.

The cartoon on the front cover is reproduced by kind permission of the Daily Express.

Andrew Thorpe

I would like to thank the University of Sheffield Research Fund for financial assistance in the writing of this article, and gratefully acknowledge information from John Hope about the security problems of 1939–40.

Richard Thurlow

Introduction

BY ANDREW THORPE

'Extremism' is at once such an emotive and loaded term that many political scientists and historians would be reluctant to employ it at all. The very concept of 'political extremism' seems to carry with it a cargo of value judgment and generalisation, often being used as a term of abuse and certainly conveying a certain odium, a bitter after-taste. It seems to imply a degree of — rather smug — satisfaction with the status quo, and a hint of suspicion as to the mental balance of those who would wish radically to change it. All this made me somewhat reluctant to entitle this volume *The Failure of Political Extremism in Inter-War Britain*. But the term, for all the reservations, can validly be used, so long as it is with a degree of caution. Basically, it is taken here to apply to those people and movements who shared a number of basic beliefs. Firstly, they either rejected parliamentary methods or else were prepared to use them only as propagandist tools in a wider struggle for power. Secondly, they wanted immediate radical changes in the country's political, economic and social structures. Thirdly, they were prepared to countenance the use of violence and 'unconstitutional' action to gain power, and, once they had gained it, the suppression of opposition, again by violent means if necessary, and the creation of a virtual dictatorship as the means of government. Clearly both the Communist party and the various fascist parties, of which the British Union of Fascists was by far the most important, were by this definition 'extremist'.

Extremism as defined here was certainly not without success in taking power in Europe between 1917 and 1940. Three types of regime emerged.

Firstly, there was communist dictatorship in Russia, set up in the aftermath of the October revolution in 1917, and established after the victory in the civil war. (There were also short-lived soviet republics in 1919 in Bavaria, Slovakia and Hungary.) Secondly, there were fascist and nazi states — Italy from 1922, Germany from 1933. And thirdly, there was a plethora of states which, although perhaps not fully 'fascist', either remained, or turned away from, democracy towards authoritarian regimes of the conservative right. Lithuania, Poland, Spain, Portugal, Austria, Hungary and Yugoslavia were all in this category before the onset of world depression in 1929; the effects of the slump helped to add Estonia, Latvia, Romania, Bulgaria, Albania and Greece to their ranks. By the later 1930s, outside Scandinavia and what are known today as the Benelux countries (Belgium, the Netherlands and Luxembourg) only Britain, France, Czechoslovakia, Switzerland and the Irish Free State could still claim reasonably to be parliamentary democracies. And even here, extremist movements were often strong. In France, 6 February 1934 saw what many took to be a fascist bid for power, as right-wing demonstrators rioted in Paris and police only narrowly averted an assault on the chamber of deputies. Two years later, the communists were supporting the popular front government of the socialist Leon Blum, implying an apparent success for the far left. In Belgium, the fascist Rexists under Leon Degrelle seemed a substantial threat in the mid-1930s. And Scandinavia, where there was a strong fascist movement in Finland and a weaker one in Sweden, was also not immune.

This volume seeks to answer the question of why, given this spread of extremism in Europe, Britain remained a parliamentary democracy with communist and fascist movements scarcely able to elect a single MP, and counting their membership in hundreds and thousands rather than in hundreds *of* thousands. The four essays which follow look at the problem in primarily political terms. I discuss the role of the Labour party in frustrating the extreme left, and Bruce Coleman similarly discusses the Conservative party in relation to the extreme right. Why did these parties remain committed to constitutional, parliamentary methods, and why did that line prove broadly acceptable to the constituencies they were addressing? The failure of the extremists is also tackled from the point of view of the Communists and Fascists themselves. Harry Harmer focusses on the Communists' most 'successful' venture, the National Unemployed Workers' Movement, in order to explain their disappointment, while Richard Thurlow concentrates on the most successful party of the extreme right, the British Union of Fascists, and discusses various interpretations as to why its aspirations came to naught. It might be objected that this is an excessively narrow approach; that other extremist groupings should also be covered, such as the Trotskyite 'Balham Group' on the left, or the Imperial Fascist League, led by the virulently anti-semitic retired camel vet, Arnold Leese, on the right. The answer is surely that such groups were even smaller and less sucessful in gaining support than the CPGB and the BUF. If the Communist party and the British Union could not succeed, then no extremist movement could. The papers in this volume treat the subject from most angles, and it would not do for this Introduction to pre-empt the issues they discuss. On the other hand, certain wider issues need to be tackled to explain why Britain was less susceptible to extremism than most of her European neighbours.

Extremist systems of government could replace the old order for a number of reasons. Firstly, invasion by a foreign power might lead to the installation of a new regime. This was to be the case, for example, in Norway during the Second World War, when the invading Germans foisted the Quisling regime onto the country. After 1945, the nations of eastern Europe rapidly gained single-party Communist dictatorships at the prompting of the USSR, which had invaded them in the latter part of the war. Between the wars this was never likely in Britain, although the invasion scare of 1940, touched on in his article by Richard Thurlow, suggested an acute awareness of the dangers of a puppet dictatorship being forced on the country should it be defeated. (The Duke of Windsor's suspected willingness to retrieve the throne under such circumstances was one reason for his exile to the Bahamas as Governor-General in 1940.)

Secondly, demographic and economic dislocation could so destabilise nations as to make them more vulnerable to communism or fascism. These points can be illustrated by comparison with Russia, where the communists took power; with Germany, where the nazis took power; with Italy, where the fascists took power; and with France, which although not succumbing to extremism before 1940, had fascist and communist movements far more powerful than did Britain.

The demographic impact of the Great War on all these countries was apparent, but Britain's total population deficit (including military losses, excess civilian or war-induced deaths, and wartime birth deficits) was relatively light (see Table 1). This is not to say that the British felt that they had got off lightly from the war: such a claim would be facile. The comparison for them was not with Russia in the 1910s, but with their doubtless rosy perceptions of Britain in the 1900s. Nevertheless, the severe economic and social dislocation implicit in the other nations' higher figures would not affect Britain so deeply.

Similarly, inter-war migration trends were not so dramatic for Britain as for some other countries. Immigration and the reactions to it have

Table 1.
Estimated Population Deficits as a Result of the First World War.[1]

Country (pre-war boundaries)	Total deficit of population (000)	Deficit as % of pre-war population
UK	1,788	3.9
Italy	2,735	7.6
France	3,074	7.7
Germany	5,436	8.0
Russia	26,000	18.5

caused social dislocation at various times in British history. These included Irish immigrants from 1800 and especially during the famine of the 1840s, the eastern Europeans who came to be seen as a political problem in the 1900s, and New Commonwealth immigration from the 1950s onwards. The inter-war years, by contrast, saw no generally noted immigration. Certainly people continued to enter Britain from outside, and from 1931 they were exceeding the number emigrating in peacetime for the first time since records began. But the numbers were low in absolute terms — only around a third of the Edwardian figures — and in most parts of the country the newcomers were assimilated with relative ease. In many ways, the inter-war period represents an anomalous stage in recent British history in terms of immigration.

This can be contrasted with Germany in the period between the end of the war and 1933, when Hitler came to power. Except in 1923, every year saw a considerable excess of immigrants over emigrants. And there was also a qualitative factor, since many of those returning came or had recently come from the former German colonies. This created a fairly articulate section of the population whose social status had clearly collapsed, exaggeratedly nationalistic and bitter at defeat in the war, and ready to believe stories of a 'stab in the back' because they had not, in many cases, been in Germany to see what had really been happening. In addition, many of the immigrants were refugees from the turmoil in eastern Europe occasioned by the Great War, the Russian Civil War and the Russo-Polish War. Many were Jews and, unlike the native German Jews, unassimilated. Much nazi rhetoric during the 1920s blamed such highly identifiable Jews

---

[1] D.H. Aldcroft, *From Versailles to Wall Street, 1919–1929* (Harmondsworth, 1977), p. 15.

for economic and moral problems: insofar as it could use Jews as scapegoats, it was using to a large extent the most recent immigrants. No such opportunity was afforded the extremists in Britain, hard though the British Union tried in the later 1930s. More broadly, the fall in emigration from the peasant societies of southern and eastern Europe, resulting at least partly from restrictive new American immigration laws, put more pressure on the land and so destabilised the nascent politics of the 'successor states' created in the peace settlements of 1919–20.[2]

Economic dislocation could also give an impetus to the development of political extremism; again, taking the period as a whole, Britain was not so severely affected as other European powers, like Germany, Russia and France. Firstly, the Great War and its aftermath caused less economic dislocation for Britain than for many of the combatants. Parts of France, Belgium and eastern Europe, especially Russia, suffered considerable physical damage under enemy occupation and as the main battlefields. Two per cent of France's land surface was laid waste, and, insofar as these areas had provided 20 per cent of her crops, 65 per cent of her steel output, 70 per cent of her coal output and no less than 90 per cent of her iron ore output, the dislocation was great.[3] Germany and Austria, like Britain, suffered less in this sense, but unlike Britain, they faced severe shortages of food and raw materials as the result of naval blockade, and this was bound to leave physical and emotional scars. The experience of Russia in these years, meanwhile, combined physical devastation with privation to such an extent that economic activity all but ceased and cannibalism had to be practised to support life in some areas. Relative to this, Britain came off lightly indeed, and wartime privations were soon overlooked as she moved rapidly into a short-lived boom in 1919–20. Although the boom broke in mid-1920, to such an extent that twelve months later she was experiencing a recession more severe than either 1929–32 or 1981, by that time many of the potentially dislocating factors at the war's end, such as demobilisation, delayed industrial disputes, and governmental preoccupation with the diplomacy of peacemaking, had been overcome. And by adopting a vigorous deflation policy, the British government ensured that what was to happen shortly in Germany would not happen in Britain.

High inflation can have serious adverse effects on the attitude of ordinary people towards the government or regime under which it occurs. This

---

[2] For figures, see B.R. Mitchell, *European Historical Statistics, 1750–1970*, (1975), pp. 142, 144.

[3] Report by G.B. Ford of the American Red Cross, Dec. 1918, printed in S. Pollard and C. Holmes, *Documents in European Economic History* (3 vols., 1973), III:51–2.

was certainly the case with Germany — most spectacularly — in the early
1920s. The inflation of 1923, when prices rose ultimately to one million million times their pre-war level, wiped out savings and left many Germans in
danger of starvation. The rentier class, therefore, living off fixed unearned
amounts (rent, interest) was especially hit. The national bank became preoccupied, not with high policy, but with the mechanics of distributing the
endless supply of new banknotes. 'Wages were paid daily and prices rose almost hourly,' and 'consumers rushed to spend, since delay could make their
cash worthless.'[4] (Significantly, the immediate aftermath of the inflation,
in November 1923, saw the Munich *Putsch* in which Hitler and Ludendorff
made an abortive attempt to overthrow the Bavarian state government as
the prelude to a march on Berlin, in the supposed manner of the Italian
fascists' March on Rome a year earlier.) Although the financial situation
was then stabilised with foreign help, and the Weimar Republic settled into
a period of prosperity, the bitter memories of the inflation remained, and
for many the Republic was irredeemably flawed.

Inflation also hit a number of other European countries at the same
time: Austria (which was to become quasi-fascist in 1934), Hungary and
Poland (both of which became authoritarian states), and, of course, Russia,
where the communists were shaken to such an extent that they had to
retreat with the new economic policy (NEP) in March 1921. Britain did
not suffer such dislocation between the wars. There were periodic fears that
she would — the fear of inflation was a significant factor in the formation
of the National government in 1931 and its policy thereafter, while during
the general election campaign of that year some use was made by National
candidates of 1923 German banknotes to show what they said would happen
in the event of a Labour victory. But after the post-war boom, deflation
was more of a problem in inter-war Britain. Prices peaked in 1920, but fell
dramatically between then and 1922, before falling slowly until 1933 (the
cost of living index, taking 1929 as 100, was 124 in 1918, 152 in 1920, 112
in 1922, and 85 in 1933). Prices then rose but, again taking 1929 as 100,
the cost of living index only stood at 96 in 1939. The general trends in
wholesale prices were broadly similar.[5] Deflation poses its own very real
problems. But it emphatically does not alienate the potentially powerful
rentier class. Prices fall, yet the rentiers continue to be paid at high rates of
interest. The chances of a party of the extreme right utilising middle-class
discontent or misgivings are consequently reduced.

Similarly, the 'downward stickiness' of wages in inter-war Britain has

---

[4] *Ibid.*, III:258.
[5] Mitchell, *European Historical Statistics*, pp. 739, 746.

been much lamented by right-wing economists and economic historians, but it did help to increase real wages for those in work and so mitigate trade union militancy. Again, the indifferent success of moves to 'rationalise' British industry may have had adverse long-term economic consequences, but it did mean that, in the short term at least, unemployment was not as high as it might otherwise have been. By contrast, the Germans were very successful in spectacular rationalisations between 1925 ands 1930, with a resultant loss of around two million jobs. These losses were not too disastrous while the economy continued to boom, but were obviously felt as soon as it moved into recession. If the cartels formed by these rationalisations 'subsequently formed the backbone of the Nazi economic machine', then it ought to be added that it was probably with the help of many of the workers thus displaced that it became a *Nazi* machine at all.[6]

Indeed the relative flatness of Britain's inter-war economic performance helped relatively flat politicians like Baldwin and MacDonald retain control. This may seem a strange statement to readers accustomed to stories of slumps, 'the hungry thirties', means tests, long-term unemployment in a Britain where everyone lived in Jarrow or was on the road to Wigan pier, of 'an enormous wastage of human resources during two decades of peace'.[7] Yet compared with most of continental Europe, Britain's experience *was* undramatic. This can be seen to a limited extent in the indices of industrial production for various countries. While it would be facile to read too much into these figures, a number of points can be made tentatively. The development of extremism in France in the 1930s was helped by the economic contrast between that decade and the very much more prosperous 1920s. The same was true to a lesser extent in Austria, which turned to clerico-fascism in the early 1930s. The extremity of the recession in Germany, after a fairly sustained degree of prosperity in 1927–9, helped extremism there. By contrast, economic activity in Britain (and still more, Sweden, which also retained parliamentary democracy) was far steadier. Before 1932–7 there was no period of sustained improvement; even the late 1920s' boom was punctuated by downturns in 1926 and 1928. The undulations of the graph were far less dramatic: and the widespread knowledge that conditions were worse in, say, Germany and the USA in the early 1930s tended to foster a degree of conservatism in Britain. The much-lamented fact that unemployment in Britain never fell below a million between 1921 and 1939 made for more stability than if the depression of 1929–32 had followed a

---

[6] Aldcroft, *Versailles to Wall Street*, p. 209.

[7] C. Webster, 'Health, welfare and unemployment during the Depression', *Past and Present*, 109 (1985), p.229.

period of full employment.

Extreme right movements tended to play on the decline of their nations. In Germany, this was easily done, given the perceived severity of the Treaty of Versailles. In Italy, D'Annunzio and Mussolini railed against the peace treaties which seemed to make their country, in theory a victor in 1918, in practice one of the vanquished. In Britain such arguments were far more difficult to deploy. She had won the war and done so well out of the peace treaties that 1921 saw the British Empire at its maximum extent. Throughout the inter-war period there was a rather complacent sense of national superiority, exemplified by the defeat of the General Strike in 1926, the victory of the National government at the 1931 general election, and the appeasement foreign policy of the later 1930s. True, there were grouses over India, over imperial policy generally, and on a whole host of other issues. But the apparent success of conservative 'good sense' in these crises suggested to many right-wingers that when she put her mind to it Britain could still show the foreigner how to behave in a tight spot. This is certainly not to agree with them. But the important point was that they could believe it. And even on imperial policy, the National government's liberal policy in the 1930s could be set against its adoption of tariff protection and imperial preference, which those same right-wingers tended to see as conducive to national greatness.

Constitutional paralysis was another factor helping the development of extremist movements in other countries. In Britain it was less of a problem, partly because of the electoral system's tendency to give governments an overall majority in parliament, and partly because of the concentration (as opposed to separation) of powers in the British constitution in the hands of the Prime Minister and cabinet, accentuated since the abolition of the House of Lords' veto in 1911. This can be compared with the multi-party chaos of Weimar Germany, towards the end of which chancellors were only able to rule by emergency decree; and with the earlier confusion in Italy, where in the face of severe social and industrial unrest in July 1922 no-one could be found to form a government. Luigi Facta resigned on being defeated in parliament; and the premiership was then offered to, and refused by, Vittorio Orlando, Enrico de Nicola, Ivanoe Bonomi, Filippo Meda and Giovanni Giolitti. Although the peak years for strikes had been 1919–21, 1922 was still heavily punctuated by disputes and this kind of governmental confusion — at the end of which Facta was finally prevailed upon to return — fatally discredited the parliamentary regime in the eyes of many Italians. Within months, Mussolini was Prime Minister.

It would not do to underestimate the potential flashpoints in inter-war British history. Six can be identified: the period of industrial unrest,

1919–21; the formation of the first Labour government, 1924; the General Strike, 1926; the second Labour government and economic depression, 1929–31; the 1931 crisis; and the crisis over unemployment benefit in 1935 (discussed later by Harry Harmer). Yet in most of these cases (as Harry Harmer shows in relation to 1935) the 'threat from the left' was fairly strictly limited to the defence of wage or benefit levels alone. Similarly, the extreme right-wing reaction which might have followed, say, the election of a Labour government or the General Strike could be subsumed (not invariably without difficulty) in the Conservative party and a reliance on the working of the British constitution, as Bruce Coleman points out in his paper.

Two broader factors might be discerned from much of the foregoing. Firstly, Britain's geographical position and island status undoubtedly helped insulate her from continental developments for all sorts of reasons — safety from invasion, and consequently less devastation due to the Great War, greater difficulty of immigration, continuity of frontiers and hence of political institutions (although a caveat about Ireland should be entered), and so forth.

Secondly, it might be argued that there is a fundamental, inherent, moderation or, putting it in very liberal democratic language, 'decency' about the British that makes them unreceptive to political extremism. This is the line of a number of observers, but was most popular among those whose parameters were defined in the heady days of prosperity, 'consensus politics' and 'you've never had it so good' in the period between the end of the Second World War and the crises of the early 1970s. Thus Henry Pelling partly explained the development of the Communist Party of Great Britain by saying that at first 'the membership consisted, to a remarkable degree, of persons of non-English origin'.[8] Explanation enough! Similarly, A.H. Birch could write in 1967 as a political scientist that the British system of government was 'a well-liked and appropriate system of government for Britain because it embodie[d] and exemplifie[d] many of the values which govern[ed] the British people in their daily lives'.[9] Why? Because:

> It ensures political stability; it protects the liberties of the subject; it satisfies British ideas about justice and fair play; it provides strong (if unimaginative) leadership; it excludes all but the most trivial forms of corruption; it gives all sections of the community a reasonable chance to express their views and protect their interests; it reacts with predictable slowness to changing situations and deals with new problems

---

[8] H. Pelling, *The British Communist Party: a historical profile* (1958), p. 15.
[9] A.H. Birch, *The British System of Government* (1967), p. 279.

> in a predictably pragmatic way; it provides serious punishments for dishonesty or indiscretion but only the most mild forms of penalty for inefficiency. [10]

There may be something in this, but it seems more difficult, writing from the perspective of the late 1980s, to accept it. Many of the trends of British history assumed to be dead in the highly aberrant 1950s and 1960s — political and industrial violence, high unemployment, downward pressure on public expenditure, concern to limit welfare provision, racial tensions, obvious social inequalities — have returned. To argue that extremism failed between the wars because the British were and remain 'jolly good eggs' (implied in Baldwin's statement that Mosley was 'a cad and a wrong 'un') seems rather dated and hollow. Generalisations about 'the national character' are probably best left out of consideration when discussing the reasons for the failure of political extremism in inter-war Britain.

Security from invasion, economic and demographic factors, the maintenance of Britain's self-esteem, and a workable constitutional system all helped Britain to avoid communism and fascism between the world wars. It is now time to consider the issue in more specifically political terms.

---

[10] *Ibid.*, pp. 278–9.

'The Only Effective Bulwark

Against Reaction and Revolution':

Labour and the Frustration of the Extreme Left

BY ANDREW THORPE

Introduction

One factor seen as helping Mussolini and Hitler to power in Italy and Germany respectively was the disunity of the left-wing opposition and, specifically, the weakness of moderate socialist parties. In Britain, the Labour party — an amalgam of trade unionists, socialists and social reformers — dominated non-Conservative politics throughout the inter-war period, while the Communists remained weak and marginal. How far and why was Labour an obstacle to the development of political extremism in Britain between 1918 and 1939?

The Labour party had fared indifferently before 1914. Long-term social and economic factors, together with the imminent extension of the franchise, were all likely to help it at some stage; but it was the war, and the consequent Liberal crises, which propelled Labour upwards in the short term. The result of the 1918 election was disappointing, though, with only 63 Labour seats against the victorious Lloyd George coalition. The breakthrough came in the three subsequent elections: 1922, when its best-known leaders returned to parliament; 1923, when, though not the largest party, it was able to form its first government with Liberal support; and 1924, when despite losing to a Conservative landslide, it increased its poll share and saw the Liberals collapse to only 40 seats. Though not an astonishing success, the first Labour government had passed some useful reforms, notably in housing, and seemed to have disproved the old gibe that the

party was unfit to govern. In 1929 Labour was able to form its second
minority administration under Ramsay MacDonald. After a bright start,
however, it was soon borne down by the pressures of world economic depression and soaring unemployment. The government's lacklustre handling
of the problem suggested defeat at the next election; and defeat was turned
into catastrophe when in August 1931 the cabinet split over proposals to
meet a budget deficit with cuts in unemployment benefit. The government
resigned; MacDonald formed a 'National' government, backed by the Conservatives and Liberals, and a few Labourites. The new ministry thrashed
a divided and demoralised Labour party at the 1931 general election. In
a contest fought mainly in straight fights, Labour could win less than a
third of the votes, collapsing from 287 seats in 1929 to 46. In the aftermath
of defeat Labour swung to the left, but not far enough for the now semi-
revolutionary Independent Labour party (ILP), which disaffiliated in 1932.
In 1935 the Labour vote reached a new peak, but changed circumstances
— the demise of the Liberals as a serious force — meant it won only 154
seats, leaving the National government with a majority of over 200. For
the remainder of the inter-war period, Labour was never close to power,
and few of its leaders expected to win the election due by the end of 1940.

Ostensibly, this was a meagre record. But too little can be made
of it. Unlike most of her continental counterparts, Britain was still 'a
democracy'. Labour, still a democratic socialist party, dominated the left,
while the Communist party, formed in 1920, was a marginal sect which
had elected only three MPs since its inception. Why had Labour rejected
extremism? And why had this rejection of extremism proved acceptable to
the party's supporters? The question needs to be answered on a number
of inter-related levels, covering leadership, ideology, the specific question
of relations with the Communists, and the attitudes of the constituency
Labour was addressing.

Leadership

Considering that they were often to be found preaching the virtues of com-
radeship and fraternity, Labour's inter-war leaders were a cantankerous
bunch much given to internecine squabbling and unpleasantness. Yet on
many issues this served merely to mask a considerable degree of consensus;
and nowhere was this more true than in the rejection of political extremism
and unconstitutional action.

This applied, certainly, to the men who dominated the party in the
years up to 1931 — the 'Big Five', Ramsay MacDonald, Philip Snowden,
Arthur Henderson, J.H. Thomas and J.R. Clynes. Thomas denied being

a socialist, but the others all claimed the title. What they meant by it varied. Henderson called himself a socialist after 1917–18, but his was a fairly nebulous doctrine based above all on arbitration and conciliation both at home and abroad. Though a prime mover in committing Labour to socialism in 1918, this was mainly a declaration of independence from the Liberals and a sign that Labour was now ready to organise and use the expected post-war upsurge in left-wing militancy. In practical, day-to-day terms, Henderson remained a fairly unreconstructed Lib-Labber. The most committed 'socialists' of the five were, in fact, MacDonald and Snowden. If their ideas were vague, their commitment was expressed frequently in books and speeches, and they continued, even after their split with Labour in 1931, to see themselves as socialists; but as democratic socialists, refusing absolutely to flirt with extremism. Hence the gloom with which the parliamentary leadership met the Trades Union Congress's attempt to coerce the Conservative government by the General Strike of 1926; hence also the sigh of relief with which it greeted the unions' participation in the Mond-Turner talks on industrial co-operation the following year. Throughout, they frowned on any moves towards co-operation with the Communists.

The domination of the Big Five collapsed with the second Labour ministry. Snowden and Thomas followed MacDonald into the National government; Henderson, who took over as leader, lost his seat at the 1931 election, and virtually abandoned domestic politics; and Clynes also lost his seat. By default, the party leadership passed to the veteran left-winger, George Lansbury. Here, it might be thought, was a man more sympathetic to extremism. During the 1920s he had tended to use his position on the national executive committee to protect Communists within the Labour movement. In 1921, as a Poplar borough guardian, he had been imprisoned for paying over-generous rates of poor relief. He had also visited and admired Soviet Russia. But Lansbury was not only a left socialist. He was also a pacifist and a Christian. Therefore he had no use for violent revolution or bloodshed, which were acknowledged as likely methods by the Communists. Thus any sympathy was always at arm's length.

More significant than Lansbury was the generation of leaders which came to dominate Labour politics in the 1930s and which in itself became the 'Big Five' of the 1945 Labour cabinet — Clement Attlee, Ernest Bevin, Herbert Morrison, Sir Stafford Cripps and Hugh Dalton. All were proud to call themselves socialists, and as sweeping a critic of Labourism as David Coates has given them grudging praise as being more committed to a socialist transformation than any other leaders before or since.[1] This is perhaps

---

[1] D. Coates, *The Labour Party and the Struggle for Socialism* (1975), p. 33.

to overdraw the contrast with MacDonald and Snowden. In particular, their attitudes to the use of unconstitutional action were almost identical. Morrison had been a leading anti-Communist from the start, battling hard to exclude them from the London party. For him, socialism could come only by consent, and despite the traumas of 1931 — when he briefly considered following MacDonald — he stuck to this line throughout his career. Similarly Bevin, general secretary of the Transport and General Workers' Union, was not radicalised by 1931, saying in its immediate aftermath that there was 'nothing for it but grim, determined effort and intensive and continuous educational work'.[2] Of the new generation of leaders, Cripps stood most self-consciously on the left; for him, 1931 was a truly radicalising experience. Yet even in 1933, at the height of Labour's swing to the left, he could answer his own question *Can Socialism Come By Constitutional Methods?* in the affirmative. The use of emergency powers against capitalist resistance was sanctioned, but insofar as Labour would then be in government, it would be acting constitutionally. Labour would not seize power by, nor make first use of, unconstitutional methods. 'I have always,' he wrote in 1932, 'condemned revolutionary means and the Communist movement which relies on such means.'[3] Thus even the most left-wing leader of inter-war Labour was not turning away from parliamentary methods, even at that critical juncture.

Why did Labour's leaders remain so opposed to any hint of unconstitutional action? A number of possible explanations can be dismissed. Firstly, capitalist bribery was not significant. Ben Tillett, the veteran dockers' leader and Labour MP, was probably in the pay of Conservative Central Office for most of the 1920s, and Thomas might have received money from the Great Western Railway after sustaining heavy losses in the stock market crash of 1929. But Tillett was a very marginal figure, and Thomas a declared non-socialist anyway. More subtle bribery, especially of MacDonald, has often been alleged; but long before any hint of the 'aristocratic embrace', he had advocated a peaceful, democratic transition to socialism. Having Lady Londonderry christen him 'Hamish the Hart' makes him seem rather foolish, but it made no difference to his basic political philosophy. Similarly, it is difficult to argue that personal laziness resulted in a lack of radical zeal. After all, there were occasions when a more left-wing line would have given the leadership a quieter life, as for example with Henderson at the 1932 party conference, shouted down for arguing that 'nothing

---

[2] Bevin to executive of TGWU, Nov. 1931, in A. Bullock, *The Life and Times of Ernest Bevin* (3 vols., 1960-83), I:503.

[3] Cripps to Sir Thomas Inskip, 18 March 1932, in E. Estorick, *Sir Stafford Cripps: a biography* (1949), p. 122.

had happened either to the Party or to [its] electoral position to warrant any scrapping of [its] programme or the revolutionizing of [its] methods'.[4] And indolence is a charge difficult to sustain against two generations of leaders who helped build Labour from virtually nothing. Indeed, MacDonald, Henderson, Bevin and Cripps all, ultimately, worked themselves to death.

There were two really substantial, linked explanations for the commitment of Labour's leaders to parliamentary socialism: their own backgrounds and the broader issue of the ideology of Labourism espoused by them and the movement they led.

Study of the background of the ten men included in the two 'Big Fives' is instructive. In social origin they were very diverse. Three had a public school and university education. Dalton, an economist, was the son of the royal chaplain at Windsor, tutor to the future King George V. Cripps, a scientist-turned-barrister, was the son of a Conservative MP; and Attlee, who, after qualifying for the Bar, had become a social worker in London's East End, was the son of a lawyer. Next, Morrison, sometime shop assistant and telephonist, and son of a policeman, was clearly of the lower middle class. But even those leaders born into the working classes did not fit cleanly into an industrial working-class mould. Bevin and MacDonald were the illegitimate sons of farmgirls, Thomas, of a domestic servant. Clynes was the son of an Irish immigrant gravedigger. Only Snowden and Henderson had clearly industrial backgrounds. In their own pre-political occupations, again, they worked in areas likely to breed little collective class consciousness. MacDonald was a journalist; Snowden an insurance clerk and civil servant; Bevin a carter in Bristol. Thomas, Clynes and Henderson all worked in more typically industrial settings, but even here there were strong forces against militancy — for example, the ironfounder Henderson was a butty at his works, thus clearly a labour aristocrat.

Their political background also suggested moderation. MacDonald's aim in the 1890s had been to become a Liberal candidate; Henderson had been a Liberal agent and mayor of Darlington before, with initial reluctance, transferring to Labour. Among the later leaders, Attlee joined the ILP, rather than the Social Democratic Federation, on the very grounds that the latter's outlook was based too much on class conflict and materialism. Dalton joined the moderate Fabian Society at Cambridge. One exception was Bevin, who in the 1900s joined the SDF-affiliated Bristol Socialist Society instead of the ILP because it was more revolutionary in spirit. But such an attitude would have been alien to him two decades

---

[4] Quoted in R. Miliband, *Parliamentary Socialism: a study in the politics of Labour* (2nd. edn., 1972), p. 193.

later, after years of painstaking union construction.

Moderation and a consensual approach were also suggested by the leaders' religious affiliations. Cripps was a high Anglican, Henderson one of Britain's leading lay Wesleyans — significantly, the least radical Methodist sect. On the left, Lansbury's Christian pacifism has already ben noted; while the leading left-winger of the 1920s, the Clydeside ILPer John Wheatley (Minister of Health, 1924) was castigated by Trotsky as 'first and foremost a Catholic and only then a socialist'.[5] While Trotsky was, characteristically, overdrawing the picture, such religious affiliations inevitably militated against unconstitutional action involving the possible use of revolutionary force.

Thus the background of Labour's inter-war leaders suggested two things. They were not likely to have any highly developed sense of alienation or exclusively proletarian class consciousness. Indeed, the more militant and alienated sections of the working classes, like the South Wales miners, tended to be unrepresented at the very highest level. And secondly, although leaders of middle-class origin came in for a variety of reasons, they were based far more on ethical or humanitarian grounds than on any kind of Marxist-Leninist aim of organising the workers for revolution.

Ideology

The rejection of extremism here is supported by analysis of the dominant ideological stance of the party they led. Much of Labour's socialist 'ideology' comprised little more than trade unionism, humanitarian sentiment and a belief in social justice and efficiency. But however garbled it might have been, it was seen as important by most members of the movement. Even Henderson, often portrayed as the archetypal party boss, surprised the chairman of the ILP, Fenner Brockway, in 1932 by basing his objections to the ILP's reaffiliation not on questions of organisation or discipline, but on more fundamental issues of democracy and the ILP's ambivalence about revolution.

Labour was a democratic socialist party; equal weight should be given to both terms. The 1918 party constitution committed the party to socialism for the first time. The definition of socialism, and when the transition would be made, were unclear. But one thing was transparently obvious. Whereas Marxists believed that socialism would arise from the collapse of capitalism, most Labourites believed precisely the opposite. Socialism would come about through the success of capitalism: the tax yields from

---

[5] L.D. Trotsky, *Where Is Britain Going?* (1926), p. 35.

successful capitalist industry would pay for the reforms which would lead gradually to the socialist millenium. This optimistic, progressive view naturally took a blow when, from late 1929, capitalism moved into crisis. The response of Snowden, as Chancellor of the Exchequer, was that orthodox remedies like spending cuts should be applied to restore capitalism and so improve the ultimate prospects of socialism. This seemed negative in all but the long term, and the party, trounced in 1931, lurched leftwards in the search for solutions. But from early 1933 the economy was improving, in some areas dramatically; and the view that socialism could evolve from the success of capitalism re-established itself, implicitly in the highly gradualist *Immediate Programme* of 1937, and explicitly in works like Evan Durbin's *Politics of Democratic Socialism*, written around the outbreak of war in 1939. Like MacDonald and Snowden before him, and Crosland and others after, Durbin took an optimistic view of capitalism:

> The capitalist economy is ossified, restrictionist and unjust; but it is expanding and stable... [Its] weaknesses ... are obvious. Its virtues lie in the maintenance of a most substantial rate of expansion, and in the increase in the degree of security enjoyed within it.

Labour's aim, he continued, should be 'to move with the stream of democratic history, and thus deflect the institutional trends within [capitalism] towards the construction of a new, more mobile and more consistent centralized or collectivist system'.[6] This really summed up what most inter-war Labour leaders thought about the organic relationship between socialism and the existing order.

Extremism was also ruled out by the party's total commitment to parliamentary democracy. Marxist views of the class-bias of the state were dismissed; for most Labourites it was essentially class-neutral, susceptible equally to capitalist or socialist control. Labour must seek to establish socialism by consent under the existing system for, as MacDonald argued, 'all change that is permanent must be a change of consent'. For Harold Laski, on the left, 'the true Socialism [was] a libertarian, and not an authoritarian, Socialism', and Labour's patchy inter-war performance did not cause Durbin to doubt its methods:

> [D]emocratic government is an essential principle, not an accidental accompaniment, of any just society... [T]he democratic method is an inherent part of socialism, and cannot be separated from it — any more than batting can be separated

---

[6] E.F.M. Durbin, *The Politics of Democratic Socialism* (1940), pp. 146-7.

> from cricket or love from life. They are necessary parts of a
> complex whole.[7]

The real requirement was the education of the British people in the need
for ordered change. To force the pace against the general will would be
disastrous, 'a breaking up of the old before the new was ready to take its
place', as MacDonald put it, which was 'not progress but chaos'.[8]

MacDonald's strictures reflected a real dread of extreme, unconstitutional action, showing not only ideological commitment to democracy but
also shrewd tactical awareness. Even before the Great War had ended,
Henderson was warning that excessive radicalism would breed fierce reaction, and this warning was borne out for him and many others by the rise
of fascist movements in Europe during the next two decades, and by the
tyrannisation of Soviet Russia. Seventeen years after Henderson, Bevin argued that 'if you do not keep down the Communists you cannot keep down
the Fascists'.[9] A proposed popular front with the Liberals and Communists
against the National government was condemned by the national executive
in similar terms:

> If Britain were to pass through critical times under a weak
> and indecisive Government of the 'Left' ... it is not unlikely
> that a rapid reaction towards Conservatism would take place
> and a grave risk of Fascism might arise.[10]

This might seem a little far-fetched. But continental fascist movements
had flourished when weak moderate-left governments were being harassed
by 'irresponsible' extremists strong enough to make trouble but too weak
to take power. Also, two years of weak Labour government in 1929–31 had
culminated in the election of a predominantly Conservative government on
a programme which, insofar as it included protective tariffs, was seen by
Labourites as the most right-wing in years.

There was also a more calculating motive behind this use of the threat
of extremism. It could help Labour to gain control of the political middle
ground being vacated by the declining Liberal party. In *The Aims of Labour*
(1918), Henderson, a particular exponent of this theme, argued that the end
of the war would see a rush of radical sentiment. Peacefully or violently,

---

[7]   J.R. MacDonald, *Socialism: critical and constructive* (1921), p. 265; H. Laski,
Socialism and Freedom (1925), p. 12; Durbin, *Politics*, p. 235.

[8]   MacDonald, *Socialism*, p. 173.

[9]   A. Henderson, *The Aims of Labour* (2nd. edn., Manchester, 1918); Bevin, in
Labour party, *Annual Conference Report, 1934* (1934), p. 140.

[10]   Labour party, NEC pamphlet, *Labour and the Popular Front* (1938).

extensive social changes would come about; and he warned of the dangers of violence:

> Revolution is a word of evil omen. It calls up a vision of barricades in the streets and blood in the gutters. No responsible person ... can contemplate such a possibility without horror ... Revolution ... will be veritable civil war. The prospect of social convulsions on this scale is enough to appal the stoutest heart. Yet this is the alternative that unmistakably confronts us, if we turn aside from the path of ordered social change by constitutional methods.[11]

In other words, Labour was, as he was to say even in the immediate aftermath of the 1931 election, 'the only effective bulwark against reaction and revolution'.[12] Labour publications throughout the inter-war period made this point repeatedly. Opposition to extremism was not only ideologically necessary and personally pleasing to Labour's leaders; it was also seen as a positive electoral asset.

Relations with the Communists

Given these circumstances, it was hardly surprising that official relations between Labour and the Communists were never better than poor. In the summer of 1920, various left-wing bodies came together, under strong and probably decisive pressure from Lenin and the Communist International (Comintern) in Moscow, to form the Communist Party of Great Britain. The party declared its adherence to the International and the soviet system, condemned parliamentary democracy except as a means of propaganda and agitation towards revolution, and applied for affiliation to the Labour party. This last was rejected by Labour on the grounds of incompatibility of constitution, programme and principles, and the rejection of affiliation was backed by the party conference in June 1921, with two further rebuffs being endorsed the following year. This effectively ruled out affiliation for the remainder of the inter-war period (a further application in 1935 being rejected on similar grounds). The problem now became one of candidates, members and delegates to Labour conferences. In October 1923 the NEC agreed to Morrison's proposal that local parties and trade unions be permitted to move against Communists. More forceful action came after the tenure of the first Labour administration in 1924 saw a series of disputes with Communists and the smearing of Labour with the odium of 'bolshevism' at the general election. That year's conference barred Communists

---

[11] Henderson, *Aims*, pp. 67-70.
[12] Henderson, *Manchester Guardian*, 29 Oct. 1931.

as candidates and party members. Unions could still send them as delegates to conferences, but the 1925 conference appealed to them to desist, and in 1928 a bar was imposed. By that stage, in any case, the Comintern was pushing the CPGB into a more combative stance, and the problem of Labour rank-and-file co-operation with the Communists ended with the imposition of the 'class against class' line in 1928–9. The dismal failure of this sectarian line meant Labour had few problems with Communists until March 1933, when, in the aftermath of Hitler's rise, the Comintern began to encourage its parties to work for a united front of all working-class organisations. The ILP co-operated, somewhat uneasily, but Labour issued a statement, *Democracy versus Dictatorship*, arguing that there was nothing to choose between communism and fascism — either would place British workers under 'servitude such as they have never suffered'. In October 1934 the TUC general council promulgated the 'black circulars', barring trades councils from admitting Communists or Fascists, and asking unions to enforce such bans in their own ranks. Further efforts at co-operation with the Communists, whether from the CPGB itself or from the Unity Campaign of 1937, in which the ILP and the Socialist League under Cripps also took a leading part, were rejected, as were later calls for a popular front.

Labour's rejection of co-operation stemmed partly from the factors discussed above. But there was more to it than that, namely, the Communists' tactics and the control exerted over the party by Moscow. Labour always maintained that, whatever they claimed, the Communists sought affiliation to and co-operation with Labour merely to play havoc in its ranks, fomenting discontent with the existing leadership and splitting the party. In support of such a view, Labour could always quote the comments of leading Communists, most notably Lenin's remark of 1920 that if he were a British voter he would support Henderson 'in the same way as the rope supports the hanged'.[13] And the Communists' actions added grist to the mill. In 1921, MacDonald, seen as essential to boost Labour's lacklustre efforts in parliament, narrowly lost a by-election at least partly because of vigorous Communist opposition. Similarly, many Labourites were antagonised by Communist attacks after the General Strike, the national agent noting that their effect was both to 'paralyse' the weaker-willed and to 'disgust our responsible people'.[14] Similarly, the line followed by Communists in the trade union movement — such as the formation of the National Minority Movement — alienated union leaders who had initially welcomed

---

[13] Lenin, *Left-Wing Communism: an infantile disorder* (1920), quoted in H. Pollitt (ed.), *Lenin on Britain* (1934), p. 257.

[14] Labour party, NEC minutes, national agent's report to organisation sub-committee, 25 July 1926.

the enthusiasm for dues-collecting and organisation shown by Communist officials and shop stewards. The TGWU, for example, was a highly diversified union, difficult to keep together at the best of times. The numerous attempts made by the Communists to disrupt it helped propel Bevin into thrusting anti-communism. This ability to make enemies was reinforced by the sectarianism of 1929–33, when Labour was condemned as 'social fascist' and its leaders as traitors to the working class. To move from such vitriolic abuse to whispering the sweet nothings of united and popular fronts struck most Labourites, not surprisingly, as the depth of opportunism. And the experience of the ILP in co-operating with the CPGB in 1933–4 served as a warning. By 1934 most ordinary ILPers were seeing united action as disastrous, partly because it prevented united action with Labour and the trade unions, but also because of the untrustworthiness of the Communists, who were making every effort to split the ILP to their own advantage. Some ILPers defected to the Communists; but others, as in Lancashire, departed in disgust to form a new party altogether. By the end of 1934, after eighteen months' co-operation with the Communists, the ILP was completely falling apart. It was a sobering example for Labourites to study.

Labour misgivings were also aroused by the obvious control exerted by Moscow. Right wingers used this fact with alacrity: Frank Hodges, secretary of the Miners' Federation, told the 1922 party conference that the British Communists were 'the intellectual slaves of Moscow, unthinking, accepting decrees and decisions without criticism or comment, taking orders from the Asiatic mind'.[15] But to Hodges' left, both Brockway and Margaret Cole attributed their non-membership of the CPGB to this Russian domination.

Such unease was intensified as the true nature of the Soviet regime became apparent, whether over the invasion of Georgia in 1921, the trial and execution of the Social Revolutionary leaders in 1922, the 'widespread summary executions'[16] following the murder of Kirov in 1934, or the show trials of 1936–8. Nothing came of the hope expressed by the Labour-TUC joint international committee in 1924, that 'normal conditions' and 'opportunities for the free and unfettered expression of the minority thought within the working-class and socialist movement' would soon be restored.[17] Disquiet and alarm at Communist tactics elsewhere in Europe, especially in Germany in 1932–3 and Spain in 1936–9, merely served to reinforce Labour misgivings. Meanwhile, Attlee, on visiting France in 1936, was appalled by

---

[15] Labour party, *Annual Conference Report, 1922* (1922), p. 198.

[16] TUC, general council minutes, 19 Dec. 1934.

[17] Labour party, NEC minutes, joint international committee, 22 July 1924.

the Communists' disruptive behaviour under Blum's popular front ministry, just as Henderson had been by the Bolsheviks' antics under Kerensky's provisional government in Russia almost two decades earlier.

Even during the 1920s, when there was particular pressure for co-operation with the Communists, Labour's leaders were able to block it with some ease. Partly this was due to the solid realities of Labour politics — the support of the union block votes for moderation. But two other factors helped. Firstly, there was the character of the Labour advocates of united action, in particular Cripps. Cripps had many fine qualities, but at times during the 1930s his conduct was such as almost to justify Dalton's acerbic gibe that he had 'the political judgment of a flea'.[18] For example, he did little to help the embryonic Unity Campaign when he said in November 1936 that he 'did not believe it would be a bad thing for the British working class if Germany defeated us. It would be a disaster for the profit-makers and capitalists, but not necessarily for the working class'.[19] And Cripps's wealth, and the use he made of it for political purposes suggested ominous parallels to many Labourites, as a miners' delegate told the 1937 conference, saying Cripps was 'a rich man, with rich pals around him, and they are the biggest danger to the Labour Party in this country. You will find those chaps where Mosley is before much longer'.[20] To be compared with Mosley — the rich ex-Conservative who had risen high in the councils of the Labour party before turning to fascism — was the kiss of death in Labour politics in the 1930s. Such images of Cripps made the lost cause of the Unity Campaign even more hopeless.

The party leadership was able, also, to deny there was any real need for united action to combat fascism and economic depression. Issuing leaflets and questionnaires about the BUF headed off demands for more direct action. Labour realised, after the setbacks of 1931 and still more 1935, the need to appeal to the middle ground. It did not want to become closely identified with street violence in what were, to most voters, geographically and emotionally remote parts of the country, against what was, to most voters, a fairly academic threat: taking a national perspective, for example, Dalton could dismiss Cripps's fears of a Fascist takeover as 'fantastic'.[21] Similarly, by conducting research into the needs of the depressed areas, and beginning to formulate a coherent regional policy, Labour could claim

[18] B. Pimlott (ed.), *The Political Diary of Hugh Dalton, 1918–40, 1945–60* (1986), p. 256, entry for 23 Jan. 1939.

[19] *Manchester Guardian*, 16 Nov. 1936.

[20] J. McGurk, quoted in K. Martin, *Harold Laski (1893–1950): a biographical memoir* (1953), p. 110.

[21] H. Dalton, *The Fateful Years: memoirs 1931–1945* (1957), p. 148.

that it was doing more for the unemployed than, say, the Communist-led National Unemployed Workers' Movement. The tag of a party of depression and unemployment had been attached to Labour as a result of 1929–31; it was a tag the party spent the 1930s trying to lose. After all, employment in most parts of the country was expanding, and party strategists were stressing the need to appeal to affluent voters in the South and Midlands. Finally, by maintaining — often insincerely — an air of optimism about the party's electoral prospects, they could give the impression that all would be well if only the temptation of 'fronts' could be resisted. Privately, few leading Labourites expected to win the election due by late 1940. Publicly, however, their propaganda warned that fronts would impair 'the growing strength of Labour in the country', and condemned the 'most fantastic defeatism' of Cripps for arguing that Labour alone was unlikely to win the next election.[22] In fact, Cripps was probably right. But where the NEC was right and Cripps wrong was in arguing that co-operation with other parties would cost at least as much support as it bought, and in particular that '[t]he presence of the Communists would bring some few thousand votes to the alliance; but it might well drive millions into Mr Chamberlain's camp'.[23] In the 1930s Labour was, very probably, unelectable. There were no short cuts, least of all through resorting to the kind of real or perceived extremism and class rhetoric which had helped to lose the election in 1931, or through co-operation with a small and rather discredited body whose tactics were decided in a foreign capital. The ultimate irony was that the formation of the CPGB as a section of the Communist International probably damaged the far left in Britain by, as Ellen Wilkinson argued, preventing the formation of 'a real left wing' in the Labour movement.[24] The existence of the Communist party, Beatrice Webb's 'ludicrous caricature of a revolutionary movement' made the avoidance of extremism that much easier for Labour's moderate leaders.[25]

Followers

Labour, then, was a party whose leadership and ideology restrained it from extremism, and which had little difficulty in avoiding working with the Communists, the one thing which might have moved it to the left. But in

---

[22] NEC statements, *Labour and the Popular Front* (May 1938) and *Unity, True or Sham?* (Feb. 1939).

[23] *Labour and the Popular Front.*

[24] *Daily Herald*, 6 Sept. 1924.

[25] N. and J. MacKenzie (eds.), *The Diary of Beatrice Webb* (4 vols., 1982-5), I:290, 3 Oct. 1932.

some ways this begs the question. Why, it might be asked, did rank-and-file Labourites, and still more the working class at large, accept this strategy? Some critics, on the left, have seen it as essentially a process of deception. Thus Trotsky wrote in 1926:

> Fabianism, MacDonaldism and pacifism ... are the main prop of British imperialism and of the European, if not the world, bourgeoisie. Workers must at all costs be shown these self-satisfied pedants, drivelling eclectics, sentimental careerists and liveried footmen of the bourgeoisie in their true colours. To show them up for what they are means to discredit them beyond repair.[26]

There was something in this. Certainly the use made by moderate leaders of conspiracy theories to excuse their failings — the 'Zinoviev Letter' in 1924, the 'bankers' ramp' in 1931 — was aimed partly to stem calls for the radical redrawing of party policies and strategies, and ordinary people and historians often believed them. But to explain the rejection of extremism by ordinary people so crudely is simplistic.

In an article concentrating mainly on the period before 1914, Ross McKibbin has shown convincingly that, leadership factors aside, there were three basic reasons for the lack of a strong Marxist movement in Britain: the fragmented nature of the workforce; the presence of a rich, varied and apolitical working-class associational culture; and the integration of the workers into the institutions of the state. These factors applied to the failure of political extremism in inter-war Britain.[27]

There were areas, like the South Wales coalfield, where a single industry with bad industrial relations and a high level of militant class consciousness dominated. But on the whole the British working class remained somewhat fragmented; in particular, trade unionism, a rough and ready guide to class consciousness, never amounted to half the workforce. From 17.7 per cent in 1911, it soared to 45.2 per cent by 1920, but then fell away so that by 1933 it amounted to only 22.6 per cent of all workers. Thereafter there was a slow recovery, but only to 29.5 per cent by 1938. In addition, the big advances made in trade union membership between the wars were often in the more fragmented and exposed sections of the workforce, in that general unions grew and white-collar and women's unionism spread. This diluted militancy further. The development of new industries — like motor vehicles — or areas — like the Dukeries coalfield in Nottinghamshire —

---

[26] Trotsky, *Where?*, p. 58.

[27] R.I. McKibbin, 'Why was there no Marxism in Great Britain?', *English Historical Review*, 99, 2 (1984).

where a premium was placed by employers on industrial 'co-operation' and anti-unionism combined with economic distress further to entrench moderation.

The cultural alternatives stressed by McKibbin — religion, sport, hobbies, clubs — continued to be important between the wars. True, the tendency of organised religion was to decline, but two points should be made. Firstly, Roman Catholicism expanded; and while providing Labour with many votes, Catholics were always more prone than other denominations to reactionary intercessions from above, as for example with Pope Pius XI's anti-socialist encyclical of May 1931, or the widespread advice given by priests to oppose Labour at that year's general election in reprisal for the Labour government's education policy. Concern here almost certainly moderated Labour's policy on Spain later in the decade: to have come out any more strongly for the Spanish republican government, at a time when the church was backing Franco, might have had severe electoral repercussions. Secondly, even if people stopped attending church or chapel, they rarely turned their backs on the non-extreme, consensual attitude to politics encouraged there. Meanwhile, sport and hobbies thrived. This relieved people like the head of Special Branch, who saw them as 'steadying influences' whose curtailment during the Great War had led to 'a melancholy dulness [sic] which impel[led] ... many to take up agitation as a pastime'.[28] Insofar as this associational culture was coming under threat, its assailants were improved home conditions and entertainments (like radio) which were still less likely to foster class consciousness or political extremism. Such factors were merely reinforced by the dread with which even dedicated Labourites might have greeted the workload piled onto Communist party members.

Nor did the inter-war working class feel particularly alienated from society. They were, firstly, committed to capitalism, or at least they saw no reason to overthrow it. As E.P. Thompson has written, 'the indices of working-class strength — the financial reserves of trade unions and co-ops — were secure only within the custodianship of capitalist stability'.[29] By the end of 1931, 9,538,515 people, perhaps two-thirds of them working-class, had accounts at the post office savings bank, with an average of around £30 in each account.[30] Even at times of distress, many workers were

---

[28] Sir B. Thomson, quoted in C.M. Andrew, *Secret Service the making of the British intelligence community* (1985), p. 201.

[29] E.P. Thompson, 'The peculiarities of the English', in R. Miliband and J. Saville (eds.), *The Socialist Register, 1965* (1965), p. 343.

[30] P. Johnson, *Saving and Spending: the working-class economy in Britain, 1870–1939* (Oxford, 1985), p. 96; A.J. Thorpe, 'The British general election of 1931', unpubd. Sheffield Univ. Ph.D. thesis, 1987, p. 502.

prepared to believe that capitalism would deliver better times, as could be seen in the number of unemployed workers, especially in the Midlands, who voted for the National government and Conservative protectionism in 1931. Depressed areas, even at the 1935 election, were not always safe for Labour: Jarrow, with 70 per cent unemployment, only gave it a narrow majority. And, broadly speaking, capitalism delivered between the wars, as real incomes and living standards rose, if unspectacularly. Even in the period of severe depression between late 1929 and early 1933, wages fell slower than prices. Secondly, the Labour leadership's view of the state — that it was class-neutral and guaranteed by an essentially impartial monarchy — was mostly shared by the workers. Extensions of the franchise — to all adults in 1928 — the receipt of honours by Labour leaders, and the general trend towards better industrial relations and, arguably, 'corporate bias'[31] all seemed to confirm working-class integration.

Indeed, it would be fallacious to argue that working-class moderation was imposed from above by Trotsky's 'liveried footmen of the bourgeoisie'. During negotiations about a possible general strike in 1921, and a real one five years later, Thomas was worried that his railwaymen, with their jobs and pensions at stake, might not follow his lead. And Bevin, leader of a diverse union comprising many shades of opinion, always maintained that he could not lead his followers where they would not be led; they were certainly not 'cracking their skins for a revolution', as he put it.[32] During the General Strike the TUC's emphasis on the constitutional and limited nature of the dispute was more for the consumption of anxious strikers than for a clearly hostile middle class; and it was no coincidence that Labour suffered by far its worst electoral defeat (1931) with its most radical, class-based manifesto. Labour between the wars had to try to win the middle ground; and that did not mean so much the middle class as the huge swathes of the working classes who disliked and distrusted even such socialism as Labour offered. It had to try to appeal in a city like Birmingham which, although mostly peopled by industrial workers and their families, elected only 7 Labour MPs (as against 77 Conservatives) in the 7 inter-war general elections. It would be difficult to argue that a more left-wing Labour party would have fared better there. To return to Trotsky, it seems only a slight overstatement to say that the workers continued to support the Labour leaders precisely *because* they saw them in their true colours as men wanting moderate reform within the existing system or something very similar to it.

---

[31] R.K. Middlemas, *Politics in Industrial Society* (1979).

[32] Bevin to 1928 TUC, quoted in Bullock, *Bevin*, I:401.

Conclusion

Between the wars Labour, for all its failings, blocked off the left and made the creation of a powerful extreme left party — difficult anyway — impossible. Labour's own rejection of extremism was rooted in the consensual, democratic socialism shared by its leaders and most of its followers. That was why the leadership was so keen to avoid working with the Communists, although, of course, the latter's own nature and tactics made then easier to ignore than they might otherwise have been. This moderate line was not imposed by a treacherous leadership on a duped rank-and-file which would have preferred more unconstitutional action; far from it. The leaders understood pretty well the hopes and fears of their constituents, the majority of whom were never faring so badly under capitalism as to want to rush headlong into a violent revolution the result of which no-one could have predicted. In that sense, there was nothing at all accidental or fortuitous about Labour's frustration of the extreme left. After all, even Marx had accepted that socialism might be reached without revolution in Britain.[33]

But perhaps the greatest contribution made by Labour to the frustration of extremism in inter-war Britain was that, on the whole, it knew its own limitations. Unlike, say, the Italian left in the early 1920s, it did not make the fatal mistake of acting strongly enough to stir up the latent power of the extreme right while being too weak to make a serious bid for power. Labour provided no more of an opening for the extreme right than it did for the extreme left. In that sense, it might well be argued that it was 'the most effective bulwark against reaction and revolution'.

---

[33] D. McLellan (ed.), *Karl Marx: selected writings* (Oxford, 1977), pp. 594–5.

The Failure of the Communists:

The National Unemployed Workers' Movement,

1921–1939: A Disappointing Success

BY HARRY HARMER

My approach to the failure of the Communist party will be to examine its activity in one area — the attempt to organise the unemployed in the National Unemployed Workers' Movement. This seems a useful approach for three reasons. First, unemployment was perhaps the central problem in inter-war domestic politics and one with a direct impact on the trade unions. Second, the Communists saw unemployment as an issue providing the opportunity for direct political influence within the Labour movement. Finally, it was — numerically at least — one of the most successful Communist activities. In the two decades of its existence half a million individuals became NUWM members.

The Communist party had been created to lead a socialist revolution in Britain. The party intended to teach the working class that militancy and agitation promised greater rewards than traditional trade unionism and reformist parliamentary socialism. It took the October revolution as the model and saw part of its role as defending Soviet achievements. The party's problem was that it pitched its appeal to an organised working class largely loyal to a Labour movement which continued to offer, industrially, the possibility of concessions from employers and, politically, the promise of a majority Labour government. Andrew Thorpe has outlined the successive tactical positions taken by the Communists to counter this obstacle and the consistently successful Labour leadership exclusion of Communist influence. An initial revolutionary enthusiasm prompted the party's foundation. As the radical wave ebbed in the early 1920s, it turned to the united front — working to build alliances with the Labour and trade union left. Then, from

PEB—C

1929, came a retreat to an exclusive radical bunker, denouncing reformist
socialism and trade unionism as 'social fascism' and 'worse than fascism'.
Finally, in response to the rise of Hitler, came a return to the united front,
broadening out in the popular front period to encompass the liberal middle
class in the defence of democracy and the Soviet Union.

The Communist party was persistently weak: 4,000 strong at its foundation in 1920, falling to 3,000 by the end of 1924. A brief blossoming came
in the excitement of the General Strike, with 10,000 members late in 1926.
Then decline until, at the political crisis of 1931, the party could claim
only 3,000 members, the majority of whom were unemployed. Membership
climbed with the rise in Europe of an increasingly aggressive fascism, the
outbreak of war in Spain and the fear of a wider conflict: from 8,000 in
1935, 11,500 in 1936 and, shortly before the outbreak of war in 1939, to
almost 18,000.

Behind all this lay the shadow of mass unemployment, never below a
million between the wars, over two million in 1921 and three million at the
trough of the depression in 1932. For the Communist party mass unemployment appeared to offer both a threat and an opportunity. At its onset in
1920, the Communists argued that mass unemployment threatened the authority of the unions, which they condemned for making no efforts to keep
the unemployed within the Labour movement. With the link ended, the
Communists said, employers would seize the opportunity to break strikes,
reduce wages and further weaken industrial organisation. But it was here
too that the Communist party saw its own opportunity. 'Communists must
realise,' the Comintern said in July 1921,

> in present circumstances the army of the unemployed is a
> revolutionary factor of immense significance, and they must
> assume the leadership of this army. Exerting pressure on
> the trade unions through the unemployed, Communists must
> bring fresh life into the unions and hasten their emancipation
> from their treacherous leaders.[1]

The objectives were three-fold. Local organisers would attract members by acting as unemployed shop stewards: offering advice on benefits and
relief, providing representation at appeals. Under Communist influence, the
unemployed would agitate for improved benefits, refuse to accept low-paid
work and join strikers' pickets. In this way those in work would be encouraged to greater militancy confident that unemployed organisation protected
a vulnerable flank. As the militant momentum developed, trade unionists

---

[1] J. Degras, *The Communist International 1919-1943: Documents* (3 vols.,
Oxford 1956), I:250.

could cast aside their reformist leaders and turn to revolution. The state, financially weakened by the expense of maintaining the unemployed, would totter. The alternative, as a joint TUC/Labour party conference on unemployment in February 1921 suggested, was to wait for a Labour government. Hannington, the Communist who emerged as the unemployed leader, accused the Labour movement of deserting the unemployed. 'We have to rely upon our own strength and authority.' His organisation in London issued an apocalyptic manifesto warning the government 'the day of reckoning will come — and nobody knows how soon' — and called a conference for 15 April 1921.[2] Out of this came the National Unemployed Workers' Committee Movement. (The word 'Committee' was dropped from the name in 1929.)

A brief word on the form organisation took. At the base were local committees, later renamed branches, built around a labour exchange. Three or four branches were grouped in district councils to co-ordinate activity in their area. A national administrative council meeting quarterly in London, made up of district council delegates and full-time officials, oversaw policy and national activity between annual conferences. Local organisers were invariably, and national leaders always, Communist party members. The movement was initially financed by collections and — the intelligence service alleged — funds from Moscow. In 1922 a national membership card was introduced and members paid a penny a week in dues, a proportion of this going to each level of the organisation.[3]

Both the name chosen and the date of foundation are significant. The name was a clear echo of the now-fading Shop Stewards and Workers' Committee Movement. The date became known as Black Friday. The Triple Alliance of miners, rail and transport workers had promised mutual aid in any industrial dispute. The fifteenth of April was the day this promise was to be fulfilled: the rail and transport unions withdrew, leaving the miners to go on to defeat alone. Here, the Communists said, was the evidence of union leadership treachery.

The recurring problem for the Communists was how far the unemployed themselves were willing to be taken. There were some cases of movement members joining picket lines. In London in the winter of 1920–1 unemployed engineers — unemployed organisation was initially strongest among the engineers — had occupied workshops to protest against over-

---

[2] *Out of Work*, No 1.

[3] For details of organisation, finance and membership see H.J.P. Harmer, 'The National Unemployed Workers' Movement in Britain 1921-1939: Failure and Success', unpubd. London Univ. Ph.D. thesis, 1987.

time being worked. But a conflict soon emerged between what the Communists wanted and what the unemployed wanted from organisation. *Out of Work*, the unemployed movement's newspaper, admitted that most London members' interest extended only as far as immediate problems of relief. 'Whilst we recognise that this is essential under the existing circumstances, we must not forget that charity will by no means solve the question of unemployment.'[4] Successive issues contained reports of appeals activities and articles on changes in benefit regulations, all intended to attract members. But once the individual grievance was dealt with the member tended to drift away. It was a problem the Communists never resolved. As a result the movement was a cardboard front: dedicated Communist leaders claimed mass support from the unemployed, that they were the voice of the unemployed; behind them lay a shifting membership with, as they were only too well aware, no political interest.

Where the opportunity for street agitation existed, as in 1921, the Communists were easily outmanoeuvred by the government. Though most workers were by now included in the national insurance benefits system, payments were limited to £1 a week, with no allowance for dependants. The Communists encouraged the unemployed to 'Go to the Guardians', the Poor Law authorities, and demand extra payments which, in the case of a family, would double or treble the amount received. The intention was to protect wage levels and to weaken the state financially. The elected guardians, closely linked to their communities, were more open to sympathy and intimidation, and appeared to the Communists to be the government's weakest point. If, as *Out of Work* No 17 said, the demands were met 'we shall have travelled a very long way towards bringing about the abolition of capitalism, we shall have struck at the very roots of capitalist society'.

Lloyd George's Coalition government — alarmed by the persistence of mass unemployment, but confident it would soon resolve itself — appeared to ride the crisis with ease. In June 1921 benefits were reduced from 20 shillings (£1) to 15 shillings (75p) a week. But in October the government introduced allowances of 5 shillings (25p) for adults and 1 shilling (5p) for each child and extended the benefit period a further 22 weeks. The object was clearly to shield the guardians from further demands and to undermine the Communist attempt to take the argument onto the streets. The Communists, however, remained hopeful. *Out of Work* declared:

> Realising that the present agitation is only a means to an end, you must go forward with these demands with an ever increasing persistence, using them as a medium through which the

---

[4] *Out of Work*, No 1.

unemployed must be educated to understand their position
in society.

But the confidence of Mond, the minister responsible for overseeing Poor
Law administration, that 'a very large majority of the Boards of Guardians
throughout the country will stand firm' appeared justified.[5]

The Movement called on what it claimed were 300 committees to turn
out in a nationwide 'week of agitation' to protest against the benefit reduction and to force Lloyd George to meet a deputation. At most 50,000
unemployed demonstrated overall. Looking back a year later the Communists saw the granting of dependants' allowances as the turning point. A
regional organiser wrote in June 1922, '[e]ver since the introduction of that
concession, the Unemployed Workers' Committee Movement ceased to be
the menace it was'.[6]

The failure derived from the persistent frustration of any opportunity
to transform the unemployed's individual problems into a collective agita-
tional issue. A further example came in February 1922 when the benefits
extension made in October 1921 was due to expire. Special Branch reported
Communist leaflets were circulating among the unemployed claiming that
'the "dole" is to be stopped and there are indications that the extremists would welcome such an eventuality. The unemployed, on the other
hand, view the end of February with apprehension'.[7] Macnamara, Minister of Labour, extended the dole a further six weeks and advised against
reducing benefits to make up the cost, proposing instead that local officials should carry out a family means test. The reasoning was obvious: an
overall benefit reduction had a mass impact and might still invite a mass response. The means test individualised and isolated the problem. With the
announcement made, Special Branch reported that Movement leaders were
'disgruntled as they were making much capital out of the alleged discontin-
uance of benefit'.[8] Indeed, the government seemed to have weathered the
immediate crisis as unemployment began to fall, from 2 million in January
1922 to below 1.5 million in October.

Out of Work set out the Communist view with a direct honesty, one
that could serve as a commentary on the longer term relationship between

---

[5] P[ublic] R[ecord] O[ffice]: CAB 24/127, 'Unemployment and Poor Law Relief', 6 Sept. 1921.

[6] *Out of Work*, No 35.

[7] PRO: CAB 24/133, 'Report on Revolutionary Organisations in the UK', 16
Feb. 1922.

[8] PRO: CAB 24/133, 'Report on Revolutionary Organisations in the UK', 23
Feb. 1922.

the party and its class. J.H. Jackson, a regional organiser, wrote, '[r]ealising
that we are faced with an apathetic and reactionary tendency amongst the
masses, it can only be expected that the popularity of our movement will
decline'. Workers had historically been blind to their own real interests,
though he did not blame them for this.

> Because they do not respond to our call in the numbers and
> enthusiasm that we would like and desire, it is not for us to
> condemn them altogether; for they are creatures of certain
> given circumstances over which they have no control.

The unemployed, in common with the working class as a whole, were not
— Jackson concluded — motivated by idealism but by the possibility of
real gains.[9]

A shift in party tactics was being heralded. The unemployed were now
no longer called upon to agitate but to become a wedge with which the
Communists could enter the broader Labour movement. *Out of Work* called
for local Councils of Unemployed and Employed. 'Your watchword must
be ... Unite. "All in for the United Front."'[10] Unemployed organisation
remained, despite the disappointments, Communist organisation. The call
for unity demonstrated that the Communists saw a long slog ahead of them,
one in which they should develop links with the left inside the broader
Labour movement.

To symbolise the new relationship the Communists organised an unemployed hunger march. Seven were mounted by the Movement between
1922 and 1936, each ostensibly connected with unemployment and the direct interests of the unemployed, but each always more directly concerned
to bring into greater prominence party policy and the turn to a new tactical
position. The irony, for all the effort put into these activities, is that it is
the 1936 Jarrow Crusade, a non-political march, that is seen as *the* hunger
march of the inter-war years.

On the surface, the purpose of the 1922 march was to force the Prime
Minister to meet a deputation to discuss the plight of the unemployed.
In reality the aim was to place pressure on the TUC to acknowledge the
authority of the NUWCM and, by extension, to ease the progress of Communist influence in the Labour movement. By early November 1922, 2,000
men — ill-equipped as Hannington later admitted — were on the road in
columns from Scotland, the North East and North West of England, the
Midlands and South Wales. Appeals for logistical support on route were
intended to lay the basis for joint employed/unemployed committees. The

---

[9] *Out of Work* No 35.
[10] *Out of Work* No 36.

government, having announced that no deputation would be received, attempted to place obstacles in the marchers' path: denying them benefits, threatening to withdraw support from the families they left behind, using its influence in the press to turn public opinion against the march.

In London, Bonar Law — who had formed a Conservative government on the fall of the Coalition in November — persistently refused to receive a deputation and the march appeared to have failed. Disappointed, marchers began to drift away. The leaders called for replacements, insisting that Bonar Law would eventually accede to their demands. But what they were waiting for was an opportunity to meet the TUC general council. 'Honestly, comrades,' *Out of Work* asked, and it was clearly trade unionists who were being addressed,

> what do you think of the fight to date of the NUWCM? We found the unemployed a collection of whining, mumping groups, totally un-class-conscious, and material for blacklegging. We (that is all of us) have given the unemployed direction, discipline and dignity.[11]

The general council met a deputation on 20 December, expressed its sympathy and accepted a suggestion for joint NUWCM/TUC unemployment demonstrations to be held on 7 January 1923. This was followed by a further meeting to discuss future co-operation. The Communists set out their proposals at the end of January. First, the setting up of a joint general council/NUWCM national committee. Second, the TUC was to instruct all affiliated union branches and trades councils to form local committees with the unemployed under NUWCM control. Finally, negotiations were to begin at once for NUWCM affiliation to the TUC.

There was clearly an element of cynicism on both sides. The general council was not so naive as to miss the implication of the proposals. It accepted the national committee suggestion, agreed to the formation of local committees, but under joint control, and rejected affiliation. Hannington declared:

> The General Council has taken up the challenge. It cannot now turn back without black disgrace and bankrupt prestige. Our Movement will strive to keep the Trade Union movement in the front line of our and their struggle. The United Front is an important and hopeful phase in the struggle and should enormously strengthen the NUWCM.[12]

With the real purpose of the march having been achieved there was now no reason to keep it in action. On 20 February 1923 the remaining

---

[11] *Out of Work* No 48.
[12] *Out of Work* No 49.

marchers left for home by train. Progress now slowed down. The general
council had been willing — in the excitement generated by the march —
to make a gesture of sympathy. But, as unemployment continued to fall,
and as it became increasingly clear that the unemployed — protected by
benefits — posed no real threat, the Communists found their position with
the general council weakening. They turned to TUC delegates to strengthen
their hand. Here there was more sympathy. At the 1923 TUC delegates
insisted that the general council should begin the co-operation promised
the previous January.

What the TUC wanted from co-operation was clear from the title 'unemployment joint advisory committee'(UJAC). Its purpose was to suggest
how the unions might respond to unemployment. Communist ambitions
ran wider: the UJAC was the contribution of the unemployed to the
Communist-inspired united front. The unemployed, of course, played no
part in it except as a largely mythical stage army in the wings. Their
role was to enable the UJAC to operate in parallel with the National Minority Movement, the left-wing alliance within the unions formed in 1924.
Through the UJAC the Communists had apparently succeeded in finding
a place at the heart of the TUC. The next two years were spent fruitlessly
attempting to strengthen this position. Patterns of agreement between the
NUWCM representatives and left-wing general council members emerged
at UJAC meetings, though only on a rhetorical level. When what the Communists were asking for contradicted trade unionism as the general council
understood it then the proposals were firmly rejected.

How, for example, could the unemployed be kept in touch with the
Labour movement? Why not, the NUWCM said, allow them to remain
union members free of charge and encourage them to become active in the
unemployed movement? In this way the unemployed would pose no threat
to trade unionism and, as a bonus for the Communists, the NUWCM would
be strengthened. The general council rejected this as an attempt to interfere
with the policies of individual unions. Next came a renewed demand for
NUWCM affiliation to the TUC. There was a direct tactical link for the
Communists. If the first proposal increased NUWCM membership then
affiliation would enable the party to wield these numbers on the floor of
the TUC. An unemployed union might even be one of the larger unions.
Successive attempts to persuade the TUC to accept affiliation were finally
ruled out of order by the general council in 1925 on the grounds that the
NUWCM was not a trade union.

Hannington complained at his Movement's fourth conference in December 1924 that many trades councils had ignored TUC requests to work
alongside the NUWCM, a clear rejection of the Communists. Benefit con-

cessions made by the Labour government had weakened the Movement, the unemployed succumbing to what Hannington described as an 'apparently inevitable apathy'. While NUWCM representatives continued to argue confidently at meetings with general council members, their own organisation seemed to be degenerating. Only twenty committees even bothered to reply to a circular from headquarters asking for membership figures to fortify the Movement's position with the general council. Joint unemployment demonstrations in June 1924 and June 1925 were no compensation. Indeed, at the 1925 rallies the tensions underlying the united front burst into the open. Trades council representatives in Manchester complained that Communist speakers 'went out of their way to denounce most of the Parliamentary leaders of the Labour Party'. Citrine, the TUC assistant secretary, added that similar complaints had come from other areas.[13] The NUWCM took a conciliatory line and promised it would not happen again.

The UJAC now staggered on, meeting increasingly less frequently. What was the purpose of a united front which achieved nothing for the Communist party and in which many members clearly felt uncomfortable? Hannington, ironically, appeared to welcome the return of a Tory government. Once the Tories opened their attack 'we should see the unemployed coming back into the ranks of the NUWCM for protection'.[14]

That this proved to be the case could give the Communists no genuine political comfort. Throughout 1926, 50,000 members flocked into the unemployed movement, only to pass out again as their individual problems were resolved. The numbers involved were, because of their inactivity, politically irrelevant.

The General Strike in 1926 brought the strains inherent in the united front to a head. The Communists accused the Labour movement leadership of treachery. In turn, this leadership reached for greater political respectability by purging the unions and the Labour party of Communist and left-wing influence. Following the strike, trades councils were instructed to refuse affiliation to the unemployed movement and the Minority Movement. In 1928 both organisations were outlawed by the TUC.

At this point the Communists voluntarily severed their links with the broader Labour movement. The shift was perhaps logical given the failure of the united front but proved to be politically suicidal. The Labour party, delegates were told at the 10th Communist congress in January 1929, had

---

[13] TUC papers, Box T1 File 135.11M: unemployment joint advisory committee minutes, 7 July 1925.

[14] NUWCM, *Report of the 4th National Conference of the NUWCM, 6/7/8 December 1924.*

become 'the third party of capitalism'. A new leadership was imposed on
the party to guarantee rigorous adherence to the line. Hannington himself
— accused of being a 'right-winger' — narrowly avoided removal from the
party's central committee. With the election of a minority Labour government in May 1929 Hannington put the new Communist position to the
unemployed movement. Labour, he said, had formed a 'Government in
the interests of capitalism, more dangerous even than the Baldwin Government because of its ability to deceive the workers'.[15] The Scottish contin-
gent on a hunger march mounted in 1930 paraded under a banner reading,
'[u]nderclad, underfed, under a Labour Government'.

As unemployment rose with the onset of depression in 1929 — 1.5
million in January 1930, 2 million by July — the Communists saw the possibility of turning to the agitation of the early 1920s. The Labour government seemed paralysed, on the point of collapse. Soaring unemployment,
and increased disqualification from benefit, encouraged NUWM growth.
But, with no corresponding increase in party membership, the unemployed
movement was increasingly called upon to carry Communist policy into the
working class. In February 1930 the Communist International warned of
the danger of Communist influence being confined to the unemployed:

> There must be no organisation which consists entirely of un-
> employed. We must not regard the fight of the unemployed
> as a particular form of movement, for unemployment is not
> a calling or occupation. The isolation of the unemployed can
> result in splitting the working class into two separate groups;
> into those who have work and those who are out of work.[16]

How could the Communists resolve this? The new line ensured that the
NUWM was the only platform available to the party, however minimal its
political authority. The Minority Movement, purged from the unions, was
in ruins. But to preserve the fantasy of a united revolutionary working-
class struggle under Communist leadership the NUWM worked with the
remnants of the Minority Movement in a disappointing National Charter
campaign. The unemployed movement found itself carrying a weak and
isolated Communist party.

This was, of course, impossible. The unemployed who joined the
NUWM — and 36,000 did so in the course of 1930 — were not revolu-
tionaries. In November the Movement's leadership complained that most
'simply joined up and retained their membership for a few weeks'. That
this had always been the experience was ignored.

---

[15] NUWM, *Report of the 6th National Conference of the NUWM, 14/15/16
September 1929.*
[16] *Inprecorr*, 27 Feb. 1930.

By the summer of 1931 the Labour government was incapable of resolving the dual problems of unemployment and the expense of maintaining the unemployed. In August the cabinet — nudged by the TUC — divided on an attempt to reduce benefits and the government fell, MacDonald forming a National government to defend sterling by making the necessary cuts. Here, it seemed, was Communism's opportunity. Palme Dutt, the party's leading theoretician, claimed that 'the Labour movement, the old Labour movement is dying. The workers' movement, the independent workers' movement is rising'.[17] But the benefit cuts were made in October 1931 and, although recruitment to the NUWM rose, there was hardly a murmur at the labour exchanges.

Piatnitsky, a Comintern funcionary speaking at a Prague conference on unemployment in October 1931, denounced British Communists for their lack of impact. He condemned the NUWM as 'a secluded organisation of the unemployed', restricting itself to reformist unemployment benefit appeals work and making no contact with what he optimistically called the 'strike movement of the English proletariat'.[18] A British party member in Moscow analysing the NUWM complained that its leaders resembled trade union leaders:

> Just as the trade unions had a stake in the continuation of capitalism so, precisely in the same way, but unconsciously of course, the NUWM was coming to have a stake in the continuation of unemployment, which was the sole reason for its existence and which had lifted it to the authority of a legally recognised organisation.[19]

If the NUWM depended on unemployment so, it was obvious, did the Communists, most of whose members were out of work. Nevertheless, the NUWM leadership loyally attempted to take responsibility for the wider failings of the Communist party as a force for revolution. There was to be a 'sharp break' with the past. Branches were to make 'contact with the workers, not only at the Labour Exchanges, but also at the Public Assistance Offices, workers' dwellings, and at the factories'. Local 'All-In Fighting Committees' were to be built on the basis of this contact. The unemployed movement had, in short — with 60 per cent of party members unemployed — to be the Communist party. Nothing happened. Branch officials — Communists fighting the often complex appeal cases meant to attract members — had no time to build the committees; the unemployed

---

[17] *Inprecorr*, 5 Nov. 1931.

[18] *Inprecorr*, 17 Aug. 1931.

[19] M. McCarthy, *Generation in Revolt* (1953), p. 172.

members, if they even heard the instructions coming from headquarters, saw them as irrelevant to their own specific needs.

Even the means test, reintroduced by the National government in November 1931 and which the Communists were confident would be a valuable spur to agitation, proved disappointing as a rallying issue. It was a return to the failed tactic of the early 1920s. NUWM branches were to pressurise locally-elected public assistance committees into conducting a mild means test, thus making the policy unworkable. The destruction of the means test, the *Daily Worker* said, again echoing the rhetoric of 1921, would 'weaken the capitalist state financially. It would bring the revolution appreciably nearer'.[20]

The Communists were making too many assumptions about the response of the unemployed. First, the problem was confined to the long-term unemployed, those out of work for over six months. Second, they assumed a natural constituency of mass anger. In fact, in the first year of the test's operation half the applicants faced no reduction in the payments they received. In addition there were wide variations in interpretation according to the political complexion of the public assistance committee involved.

Local agitation having failed, the Communists organised a 1,500 strong hunger march in September 1932. That this took place against a background of riots on Merseyside and in Belfast, where two demonstrators were killed, increased political tension but contributed nothing to the success of Communist policy. At the psychological moment the government threw in a minor concession, one that satisfied the TUC, and ensured the Communists were denied any wider sympathy. The press stressed the dangers of Communist-inspired violence, a campaign encouraged by the party's over-inflated revolutionary rhetoric. When the marchers reached London carrying a million-signature petition against the means test they faced a massive police presence and there were violent scuffles in Hyde Park. Hannington, arrested in the course of the London demonstrations, was punished for his Movement's — and his party's — failures by removal from the central committee.

Even the Communist leaders appeared embarrassed that their influence seemed limited to the unemployed. At the November 1932 party congress Pollitt, the Communist general secretary, complained, '[t]here should be no looking down upon a comrade because he is employed. There is such an attitude in the Party. We have to kill the idea that it is the hallmark of a Communist to be unemployed'.[21] Prime Minister MacDonald, for his

---

[20] *Daily Worker*, 1 Sept. 1932.

[21] CPGB, *The Road to Victory* (1932).

part, seemed satisfied that the Communists were totally isolated from the Labour movement. 'How are we to keep the Communists dissociated from the trade unions?' he wrote to the Home Secretary in December 1932. 'Up to now we have succeeded remarkably well in this.'[22]

The Communist problem — as Pollitt implied — was how to renew the association. The rise of Hitler in 1933 and the fear of fascism provided one key. As the Nazis consolidated their power, the Comintern, wary of the dangers Germany now posed to the Soviet Union, reassessed its position. A manifesto in March 1933 urged Communists to call upon socialist parties and trade unions to build a united front against fascism, adding that 'no criticism should be directed against Socialist organisations during the period of common action'.

Richard Thurlow will go more deeply into the political significance of fascism in Britain. Whatever the reality, it was necessary for the Communists to argue that there was sufficient danger to justify a united front invitation to the Labour movement. The TUC and the Labour party immediately rejected Communist proposals. In a pamphlet entitled *Democracy versus Dictatorship* they equated fascism and communism as forms of dictatorship and drew a sharp distinction between democratic and revolutionary socialism.

In 1932 the Communists had castigated the Independent Labour party as 'the left hand of British capitalism'. Now, in 1933, the ILP — fragmented and in decline since its split from Labour the previous year — accepted the united front invitation. NUWM branches were urged by Hannington to 'set the pace' in the united front campaign. Indeed, as it was their only mass organisation the Communists had no choice but to place large hopes in the unemployed movement. Once again they turned to a hunger march to symbolise the new strategy. NUWM leaders appeared — if Special Branch reports are to be believed — initially hesitant, preferring to wait until there was some genuine sign of interest among trade unionists. Gallacher, for the Communists, accused them of cowardice.

The march, 1,500 strong, went ahead in January 1934. It was to culminate in a united front congress in Bermondsey Town Hall as the marchers arrived in London on 24 February. When the Home Secretary, Gilmour, warned of the dangers of violence and said the Communists would be responsible, the united front committee accused him of signalling approval for an attack on marchers by the police and Mosley's Blackshirts. 'The National March becomes a test for the working class movement.' If it failed

---

[22] PRO: PREM 1/129, MacDonald to Sir John Gilmour, 30 Dec. 1932.

the test then Britain would follow Germany down the road to fascism.[23]

The Labour movement was unimpressed. Trades council unemployed associations formed by the TUC in 1932 refused to support the march. Assistance on route and in London hardly extended beyond the Communists and the ILP and many ILP members were wary that the Communist party was using the united front purely 'for its own sectarian advantage'.[24] The NUWM leadership regretted how few of its own branches had applied for credentials to attend the united front conference. The conference, and a celebratory rally in Hyde Park the following day, proved disappointing and the united front remained fragile.

Then, as the Communists digested their disappointment, the unemployed, much to the surprise of both the Communists and the government, took to the streets in almost spontaneous mass demonstrations. The trigger was an Unemployment Act which restructured the benefits system. Local public assistance committee provision for the long-term unemployed was replaced by a centralised unemployment assistance board. The UAB began work in January 1935 and it soon became apparent that while 34 per cent of claimants would receive increased payments, 48 per cent would be worse off. The TUC had rejected an NUWM 'Call for Unity' against the new scales in December 1934. Equally, NUWM members showed no interest in distributing a leaflet based upon this call, indicating, headquarters complained, that 'our branches in the main are not undertaking the united front drive into the trade unions and other organisations as they should be doing'.[25]

As the extent of reductions became clear, the unemployed, together with — particularly in South Wales — trade unionists, church members, PAC officials, Labour councillors and even MPs, took up the Communist and ILP call for mass protests. In Sheffield the Labour PAC leader promised to make good the cuts and defied the government to interfere. On 22 January, Hannington led a 40,000 strong demonstration in South Wales, the *Manchester Guardian* commenting that this had caused 'great surprise and uneasiness.... The official Labour party held aloof, and the protest was organised by the numerically feeble Communist Party, Independent Labour Party and Unemployed Workers' Movement'.[26] Shocked by the extent and anger of the protests the government acknowledged its own clumsiness,

---

[23] *Daily Worker*, 5 Jan. 1934.

[24] A.F. Brockway, *Inside the Left* (1942), p. 252.

[25] Communist party archive, Hannington papers, A2d, NUWM circular to all district councils and NAC members, 4 Jan. 1935.

[26] *Manchester Guardian*, 25 Jan. 1935.

retreated, and promised all cuts would be restored in a standstill order on 5 February.

And then, as rapidly as it had arisen, the uproar subsided, leaving the Communists incapable of building on the momentum. 'In district after district,' the NUWM leadership said,

> Labour councillors and district Trade Union leaders have felt the urge to mass action from the rank and file and have joined in the united front against the Act, in spite of the persistent refusal on the part of the National Trade Union and Labour leadership to join in the United Front.[27]

This may well have been true: but only for a few days, and only on a single issue. Disturbed by the lack of political reward from the events, Pollitt blamed the NUWM leadership and party members generally for their 'lack of urgency'. When Labour and union leaders rejected united front approaches, he complained, 'too often such expressions can be heard: "Well, that was to be expected, now we can get on with our own work"'.[28] This was an extraordinarily revealing remark for Pollitt to make. The work of party members was presumably to further the party's policy.

This policy now became increasingly concentrated on ensuring the defence of the Soviet Union against Germany. It was essential, Pollitt said in October 1935, to 'support 100 per cent, and without any reservations, everything that the Soviet Union does in its foreign policy'.[29] The Soviet Union had joined the League of Nations, was concluding an alliance with France and sought closer links with Britain. Communist policy in Britain was intended directly to assist this by encouraging the growth of a vigorously anti-Fascist Labour movement. If the National government appeared indifferent to fascism — both domestically and internationally — then this was, the Communists implied, because it was itself close to fascism. With the call from the Comintern for a popular front policy in August 1935 the Communist effort became two-pronged. First, to carry militant anti-fascism into the Labour movement. And, on the basis of this to extend an appeal to the liberal middle class to join in the defence of democracy. But to expect success was grossly to overestimate the significance of the Communist party in British politics. It was also to underestimate the unwillingness of Labour and trade union leaders to tolerate the Communists.

---

[27] Marx Memorial Library, Hannington papers, AI & AII, NUWM NAC minutes, 9/10 Feb. 1935.

[28] CPGB, *Harry Pollitt Speaks: A Call to All Workers* (1935).

[29] *Labour Monthly*, Oct. 1935.

Communist influence in the Labour movement — despite some successes in South Wales — remained weak, not least because of the determination of Citrine, the TUC secretary, and Bevin, the influential Transport and General Workers' leader. In their view, building closer relations with the Soviet Union — and they recognised the value of this — did not involve encouraging what they saw as the Communist nuisance in their own movement.

For all its failings, the NUWM remained a card for the Communists to play. Members were no longer called upon to be activists — as in the revolutionary days of 1931-2 — but simply to be there as a stage army. Only organisation, the Communists claimed, held the unemployed from joining the Blackshirts out of despair. The return of the National government at the 1935 general election — despite Labour party recovery, and despite the election of a Communist MP — encouraged the Communists to greater efforts.

In January 1936 Pollitt regretted that activity against unemployment was at what he called a 'low ebb'. This was, he said, because of the division between the NUWM and the TUC unemployed associations. What was required was unity between the two, 'one united unemployed organisation identified with and part of the trades councils and the Trades Union Congress'.[30] As in the mid-1920s, the appeal was intended to influence the Labour movement rank-and-file. In November the NUWM organised a hunger march to act out the attempt, with the Communists performing a charade to cover their own role in the march. It was made to appear that the call for a march — already decided upon by the NUWM — had come spontaneously from the heart of the Labour movement in South Wales. Pressure was then to flow upwards from the rank-and-file to the TUC and Labour leadership, drawing them into recognising the march and, by implication, the united front.

At one level the charade worked. What was important was that signs of a wish on the left for a more militant anti-Fascist attitude did exist, held back, the Communists argued, by the Labour and TUC leadership. In July 1936 the Spanish popular front government had been attacked by the army and the right and civil war was now raging. The reality of the conflict was more complex than the Communists suggested but the emotional effect on the left in Britain was intense.

A reception committee for the arrival of the marchers in London included not only Communists but three left-wing Labour MPs. The NUWM's part in organising the march was minimised to such an extent

---

[30] H. Pollitt, *Selected Speeches and Articles, Vol I: 1919–1936* (1953), p. 177.

that it appeared the Movement hardly existed. The 1,500 marchers crossing England met with a greater show of local support from the Labour movement than on any previous march. At a welcoming rally on 8 November even Attlee, the Labour leader, appeared on a platform clearly — if perhaps cynically, given his attitude towards Communists — feeling the need to placate his own left wing.

What disappointed the Communists in broader political terms was the simultaneous success of the Jarrow March. It was smaller — only 307 strong — and distinctly non-political. Hannington was reported to have complained, '[t]hey have taken the butter off our bread'.[31] Why, if the purpose of a march was simply to draw attention to unemployment, was Hannington jealous? Because, it was clear, what lay behind the Communist march was not unemployment but the desire to realign the left. It frustrated the Communists to see the Jarrow Crusaders win public sympathy and so undermine their own effort.

Having shown their commitment to self-sacrificing unity on the march, the Communists now offered to dissolve the NUWM into the TUC, an offer immediately rejected.[32] 'One of the most amusing spectacles which contemporary history will reveal,' Citrine told the TUC, 'will be the frenzied attempts that are being made by the Communist movement to ingratiate itself with organised labour.'[33]

The second thrust of Communist policy was towards the liberal middle class. Unemployment and the means test remained emotive issues, with reports on the conditions of the long-term unemployed appearing with increasing frequency. The unemployed were used by the Communists to reach out not to the hard-done-by for active support — as in the past — but to do-gooders for intellectual sympathy. NUWM literature was increasingly aimed at what were seen as influential middle-class readers rather than the unemployed. Hannington's books describing conditions in the depressed areas and denouncing the National government were circulated by the Left Book Club. An anti-means test petition in March 1936 provided a further example of the shift. Collecting signatures for the 1932 petition had been intended as a means of agitation among the unemployed themselves. The 1936 petition was to help galvanise the liberal middle class. NUWM headquarters called on 'responsible members of the branch' to approach doctors, shopkeepers, clerics, journalists and what it described as 'other influential

---

[31] PRO: MEPO 2/3097, 'Summary of Jarrow March', 6 Nov. 1936.

[32] H. McShane and J. Smith, *Harry McShane: No Mean Fighter* (1977), pp. 219-22.

[33] TUC, *Report, 1936* (1936), p. 423.

people' for their signatures. 'We only want the signatures of persons of public standing.' Branch officials were ordered to keep the petition in a folder. 'Public men will not sign a scrappy document.'[34] Tactically, this was perhaps a necessary tone to take but, for reasons I find hard to explain, it leaves an unpleasant taste in the mouth.

There is no doubt, however, that such campaigns did have an impact, encouraging an influx of intellectuals and professional people into the Communist party and — where support did not go that far — generating a wider sympathy for popular front arguments. But the practical results for the Communists were minimal. At the May 1937 party congress responsibility was allocated. The Labour movement continued to exclude the Communists. Without a united front there could be no popular front. As far as the unemployed were concerned, the central committee blamed the NUWM itself. The party had been 'hampered by sectarianism inside the NUWM which our own members have not effectively tried to overcome'. A leading party member attacked individuals who, he said, had become 'immersed in detail, so that they fail not only to recruit but also to develop themselves politically'.[35] It was Hannington who was being called upon to take responsibility for Communist failure. Having been returned to the central committee as a reward for the 1935 events he was once more excluded. What this meant was that, for the remainder of its existence, the NUWM could continue being what it had in reality always been to its members — not a means of entry for the party into the Labour movement but a form of trade union fighting case by case for the unemployed.

Why was the disappointment so intense and, as often in the past, so vindictively expressed? Precisely because the Communists had always been forced to stake so much on the NUWM. For the Communists to have depended so heavily on their contact with the unemployed — it could never really be described as influence — symbolised their wider failure. The success of the NUWM, and it can be called a success, did not lay in advancing revolutionary arguments to the unemployed but in defending their individual interests as claimants. In much the same way, when industrial workers turned to Communists it was not revolutionary leaders they were seeking but competent shopfloor militants. Ultimately, only the benefits system gave the NUWM a reason for existence in the eyes of its members; but the continuation of benefits prevented unemployment from becoming the destabilising factor the Communists sought, destabilising both government

---

[34] NUWM circulars, 6 and 25 March 1936.

[35] CPGB, *It Can Be Done: report of the 14th congress of the Communist Party of Great Britain, 29-31 May 1937* (1937).

and Labour movement leadership. The political irony for the Communist party was the less it spoke of revolution the more sympathy it aroused: in the anti-Fascist popular front period and, after a false start in 1939, riding in the wake of the Soviet military effort against Germany.

48

The Conservative Party

and the Frustration of the Extreme Right

BY BRUCE COLEMAN

The title itself poses at least two problems. First, once one excludes the various Fascist groups of which Mosley's BUF (the subject of chapter 4) was the most prominent, there is no clear definition of the term 'the extreme right'. For present purposes it is assumed to include also the political territory of figures like Colonel John Gretton MP and Brigadier Sir Henry Page Croft MP, two persistent Diehard critics of centrist tendencies in their party who have been suggested as the inspiration of the cartoonist Low's 'Colonel Blimp', like the press lord Harold Harmsworth, Viscount Rothermere, like the imperial proconsul Lord Lloyd and like Admiral Hall, a former head of Naval Intelligence and sometime principal agent of the Conservative party.[1] Many others could be added, but these examples may suggest the flavour of the Tory ultra-right, which so often railed against its own official leaders, which sometimes took its dissidence so far as an institutional challenge to the Conservative party itself and which arguably had certain ideological affinities with the Fascist right. The second problem concerns the idea of failure. Though the Tory extreme right never gained control either of its own party or of national government, its experience of inter-war politics arguably fell some way short of complete failure and it probably derived more satisfaction and reassurance from events than its equivalent on the extreme left and than the term 'frustration' might suggest.

---

[1] Brief biographical details of these and other figures of the right can be found in G.C. Webber, *The Ideology of the British Right 1918–1939* (1986), Appendix, pp. 142-65, and, in some cases, in the *Dictionary of National Biography*.

The Conservative party became more self-consciously 'right' during this period, partly because a more self-conscious and ideological 'left' was arrayed against it. The advance of the Labour party, the growth of trade union membership and influence and the success of bolshevism in Russia had all encouraged this sense of identity even by 1920. Further developments in European politics, including the rise of fascism, ensured that by the 1930s 'left' and 'right' were familiar terms of political analysis as they had not been before 1914. Baldwin, discussing the squeezing out of the Liberals as a disruptive third party in 1924, saw his party as 'the Party of the Right' in contradistinction to the 'Party of the Left' (Labour). Yet this broad right, as Baldwin saw the Tories, enjoyed a notable measure of success (as normally understood) in the period and rarely needed to see itself as on the losing side. If a powerful 'extreme right' is produced by a reaction against the failure of a more broadly-based and conventional conservatism, as happened in certain other countries, the preconditions for it hardly existed in Britain. The right was never 'frustrated' enough to need its own 'extremism'.

To argue this is not to fall into that self-congratulation upon ingrained moderation which sometimes shows in house histories of the Conservative party, nor to fall for the more sophisticated argument about the strength of centrism in British politics which Brian Harrison has deployed.[2] These approaches seem to assume that 'moderation' has been a virtually innate quality in modern British politics, at least in respectable, constitutional parties like the Conservatives. Neither allows enough for the possibility that 'moderation' is, in part, the product of particular circumstances and that traditions and habits of political behaviour can be eroded when these circumstances change. One needs to examine the circumstances of the inter-war Conservative party to understand how and why it sustained a highly constitutionalist and largely moderate leadership, kept the intransigent or maverick right largely confined to the political fringes (whether those of the party itself or outside it) and scarcely needed to regard the separatist right as a serious rival or menace.

By 1914 the Conservatives, for all their recent problems, had established themselves as the broad church of the political right. As such, despite their internal strains, there was no serious challenge to them nationally. The merger of the Liberal Unionists with the Conservatives in 1911–12 had simply confirmed the position. The lessons of history and the logic of the electoral system suggested no different. Folk memories of the harsh penal-

---

[2] B. Harrison, 'The centrist theme in modern British politics', in his *Peaceable Kingdom: stability and change in modern Britain* (Oxford, 1982), pp. 309-77.

ties of schism after 1846 remained an influence on Tory attitudes and even the bitterness of the tariff reform issue after 1903 had produced no major or permanent fracture in the party. The simple majority system for elections worked to discourage the foundation of new parties and helped to convince most Tory dissidents that they were better off working to influence their party from within than challenging it from without. The failure of Henry Page Croft's National party after 1917 suggested that right-wing splinter parties would fare badly against official Conservatives. Yet the fact that the Great War confirmed more than it disrupted Conservative unity, in sharp contrast to what happened to the Liberals, owed something also to the party's successful long-term adaptation to the mass politics which had developed since the 1860s. The Conservatives, once a party identified with aristocratic influence, had committed themselves with considerable vigour to competition for the votes and seats of the 'democratic' urban constituencies. The party had adapted, not succumbed, to modernity. By the turn of the century the Conservatives' central, constituency and associated organisations were probably more 'advanced' and effective than those of their Liberal opponents.

One reason was that they were usually better financed. The Tories were able to tap a broad base of private wealth for both local and central expenditure and they would never be as hard-up as the Liberals. They had a plentiful supply of candidates able to bear their own expenses; they could pay for professional agents in many constituencies and for propaganda, usually centrally directed, on a national scale. It was not simply that the party could usually outspend its rivals and so help its own chances of success; there was never a financial collapse which left the party organisation vulnerable to the charms of one or more wealthy paymasters with panaceas of their own to peddle. Even Beaverbrook and Rothermere combined, as they were in 1930–1, could not buy the party. Nor did it need Mussolini's money as Mosley did in the early 1930s — nor, for that matter, Lloyd George's money in the 1920s. The party's broad base of affluence was arguably a factor in its stability and its resistance to 'extremism'. The party's long tenure of office in the late nineteenth century and again between the wars helped to ensure that wealth continued to be attracted to it. A party of government could offer employment, a route into parliament and, of course, honours. The 'rage for honours', as it had been labelled towards the end of Victoria's reign, fed into the party's stability and success. It helped the party to fuse successfully for political purposes wealth from business and the professions, old property and new money. Different kinds of wealth did not need separate parties of their own.

It is worth adding that this fusion of diverse economic and social interests within or behind the Conservative party had been achieved on a national basis. Before 1914 Southern Ireland had been the only part of the United Kingdom where the Conservatives and Unionists could not win seats in substantial numbers. With the exception of the Irish Nationalists — Ulster Unionism had remained closely tied to the Conservatives — there had been no splintering of the party structure as a whole and of the political right in particular on regional, ethnic or national lines. Once again this was a feature that distinguished the political right in Britain from that in certain countries in continental Europe.

The solidity of the Conservative and Unionist party as the Broad Church of the political right was not seriously disrupted by the Great War. The party suffered no major schism from its strains — of the 23 candidates put up by Page Croft's National party in 1918 only two were elected — and by 1918 it was benefiting from the prestige of victory and of patriotic duty well done. It was able to cope with the major franchise extension in 1918 partly because of Liberal divisions but also because Conservative morale was high, and the enfranchisement of women (at first largely married women over 30) proved to be no handicap to the Tories. Certainly the increasingly unhappy experience of the Lloyd George Coalition created greater strains within the party, particularly once Austen Chamberlain had succeeded Bonar Law as leader in 1921, but the 'Diehard revolt' (a self-conscious replay of that against Balfour's leadership in 1911) was fuelled more by a desire for the party's restored independence, unity and monopoly of office than by a commitment to an explicitly alternative and 'right-wing' programme. The destruction of the Coalition by a Tory party revolt in 1922 owed a good deal, indeed, to the desire of moderates like Baldwin and Bonar Law to discipline their own right wing. In the event the establishment of solely Conservative government, initially under Bonar Law, pricked the bubble of the 'Diehard revolt', rallied most of the party behind the new leadership and led to only a temporary exile for the greater part of the former Coalition Conservative leadership. Baldwin, by now party leader, had the prudence to reconcile Austen Chamberlain and his supporters to the main body of the party after the Conservative triumph in the 1924 general election, when the party won the largest *single*-party majority in British political history.

It was important that the only two periods of opposition, those of 1924 and 1929–31, were short-lived. A recent study of the second period has shown how traumatic the loss of office was for the Conservative party.[3] No doubt 'moderation', by its appeal to a broad spectrum of national opin-

---

[3] S. Ball, *Baldwin and the Conservative Party: the crisis of 1929–31* (1988).

ion, helped to produce electoral success and so office for the Conservatives. Office, though, also helped to produce and perpetuate moderation. Apart from those two short periods, the party held office, either singly or in coalition, from early 1915 to mid-1945. Significantly the nearest the party strayed to a radically unconstitutional line that could be characterised as 'extreme right' during the first half of this century was during the period from late 1905 to early 1915, which was the longest continuous period of opposition it has experienced in its whole history. From 1910 to 1914 the pressures stemming from the House of Lords and Irish Home Rule issues moved sections of the party towards a rejection of the constitutional norms which, if in government, they would have been quick to uphold. Many Tories regarded both the 1911 Parliament Act, which removed the absolute veto power from the upper house, and the subsequent Home Rule Bill as unconstitutional. Bonar Law's Blenheim speech of July 1912 virtually rejected the concept of parliamentary sovereignty and the duty of allegiance to national government, the latter being characterised as 'a revolutionary committee which seized power by despotic fraud', so that Unionists need no longer feel themselves constrained by conventional niceties. There were 'things stronger than parliamentary majorities'. During this phase elements in the party (though not always the same ones) conspired to use King George V to eject a Liberal government with a secure Commons majority, played with the idea (and even more with the threat) of military mutiny and, at the very least, did nothing to discourage the arming of Ulster volunteers for an anticipated civil war in Ireland. But the moment and the mood passed. The frustration of impotent opposition — the sense that class or ideological enemies were in power — was one the Conservatives would hardly have to experience over the next three decades. Instead the party would find itself a near-permanent party of government with all that that entailed for the gratification of its supporters and for the perspectives of a party leadership highly experienced in office. The party was to be led almost permanently from the government front bench. The sudden elevation of Baldwin in 1922–3 was the only sharp break in the continuity of the party's leadership between the wars and no-one was more committed than Baldwin to the re-establishment of constitutional (and highly conservative) 'normalcy'. The Conservatives were never to suffer disruption and division from the experience of acute failure or of impotent terror which the parties of the conservative right suffered in certain European countries. Indeed some of the fears of the period before the war were laid to rest. Except through the impact of wars, the fiscal burdens of which patriotic Conservatives were usually prepared to accept, the interests represented in the party never had to submit to 'confiscatory', redistributive and retributive taxation of the kind which the 'People's Budget' of 1909 had seemed to presage.

The legacy of the Great War left its mark on the political right in other ways. The fact that the war ended in victory, not defeat, made its main psychological impact confirmatory rather than radicalising. It tended to increase the prestige of the constitution and of the symbols of patriotism, the Crown among them, rather than undermine them. The Conservatives reaffirmed their role as the patriotic party and as the defender of an inherited (if happily adaptable) constitution and buried with little mourning many of their 'radical right' tendencies of 1910–14. Britain experienced no Versailles of the kind that helped to undermine the Weimar constitution in Germany, by depriving it of the instinctive support of basically conservative opinion, and there was no sense in Britain in the 1920s of an alien constitution foisted upon an unwilling country nor of a regime without foundations in popular consent. The war and its aftermath had also excised the problem of Ireland from the political scene, at least the problem in its virulent pre-1914 form. Ireland certainly remained a disruptive factor down to 1922 and resentment at the Coalition's search for a negotiated settlement had contributed to the 'Diehard revolt' against the Coalition, but this right-wing reaction did not prevent the settlement of 1921–2 and the creation of the Free State. The most virulent influence on pre-war Toryism — militant Unionism, especially its Ulster variety — was now shorn of its influence upon both the party as a whole and upon its leadership. The potential for major political violence emanating from Ireland and for a virtual overthrow of the established constitution in this way was gone. Ironically one consequence of the removal of most of the Irish seats from the Commons was a net gain to the Conservatives of some 55–60 seats. (The Unionists had been very much the minority in Ireland as a whole, but were now very much the majority in the remaining Ulster representation.) This gain, which, had it been achieved by then, would have put the Unionists back into office in 1910, would be of assistance to the Conservatives in dealing with the post-war three-party structure. It served as a modest compensation for the (to Conservatives) disastrous and, in the 1920's, still worrying loss of the House of Lords' absolute veto through the Parliament Act.

The third benefit which the war produced for the Conservatives as the broad right of British politics was the split in the Liberal party and the subsequent disintegration of its parliamentary personnel and its mass support over a period down to the mid-1930s. Any Liberal revival during this period was a threat to the Conservatives' hold on office, as was shown by the general elections of 1923 and 1929, when the Liberals pushed the Tories down to about 38 per cent of the national poll and about 260 seats in the Commons. The three-party structure was seen as a menace by Conservative strategists, who had learned to fear multi-party politics in the years before 1914, and they were anxious to restore a two-party confrontation as soon as possible, particularly as they were confident they could beat the Labour party. But this objective required a squeezing-out of the Liberals by a Conservative appeal to former Liberal voters, many of whom were Nonconformists. Conservatives ignored this strategy when they rejected the embrace of the Coalition Liberals so vehemently in 1922, but the failure of their party in the general election of 1923, after Baldwin had dissolved on a tariff reform platform which aided Liberal unity and which put Labour into office for the first time, taught many thinking Conservatives, not least Baldwin himself, that the party had to discipline itself to woo Liberal and ex-Liberal voters. One consequence was Baldwin's eschewal of the protection issue until forced back to it in the early 1930s. Another was the persistent emphasis on social harmony and class conciliation, on the avoidance of provocation, on a liberal direction in imperial policy, especially over India, and on disarmament and international co-operation. Here was the liberal-flavoured Conservatism which came to be seen as characteristically Baldwinian. Even the electoral defeat of 1929, when the Conservative government, fighting on the low-key slogan of 'Safety First', fell foul of a limited Liberal revival under Lloyd George, did not disguise the fact that the Conservative party was becoming (and, for electoral purposes, needed to become) a party fit for ex-Liberals to support. Much of Baldwin's rhetoric — the piety and moral exhortation of 'Peace in our time, O Lord', the call for social harmony and political magnanimity, the emphasis on simple faith and trust — was redolent of the respectable kinds of Liberal Nonconformity of earlier years. Baldwin's strategy of neglecting his own right wing in order to appeal to the disintegrating centre of British politics was bound, however, to add to the problems he experienced when his party found itself in opposition in 1929–31.

Another gain from the war period for the Tories had been the replacement of the Liberals as the main opposition by the Labour party, though initially many Conservatives had been far from reassured by the almost simultaneous triumph of socialism seemingly represented by Russia's Bolshevik Revolution. But if the rise of Labour, with its 1918 constitution's vague commitment to 'socialism', was seen as a threat by many of the propertied interests represented in the Conservative party, it was also an asset in political terms. The Conservatives could profitably present themselves as the bulwark against socialism and bolshevism and expect to reap the electoral benefits. A 'socialist', union-dominated and (according to Tory propaganda) dangerously fellow-travelling Labour party was an easier opponent than the pre-1914 Liberal party with its Irish allies and satellite Labour party had been. The benefits of an assertively anti-left stance to the Conservatives were apparent in 1922, in 1924 (when the Zinoviev Letter added edge to the confrontation) and in the National government's elections of 1931 and 1935. This aspect was less prominent in 1923 and 1929 and significantly the Conservatives performed worse in these elections.

At the same time the form and the presentation of the resistance to the left needed care. The most rewarding line was likely to be an assertion of traditional values like social harmony, class co-operation, political stability, constitutional order and patriotism, rather than of more radical ideological positions like those some of the Tory right wanted to espouse. (Even the Tory right was divided, however, between traditionalists and a more self-consciously radical element.) But there were always elements in the party that wanted a more aggressive confrontation with the left and they had their opportunity after the General Strike of 1926. The hardliners were now able to force upon a somewhat reluctant cabinet the Trade Disputes Act which they had sought earlier in the decade. William Joynson-Hicks, the Home Secretary, was able to give a freer rein to his anti-bolshevism (the Arcos raid was one result) and to his conviction that moral and political degeneracy in general should be resisted. There was, however, never to be an all-out assault on the left in either its political or its industrial aspects. The Trade Disputes Act hindered both the Labour party and its affiliated trades unions but it did not shackle them. The relatively modest response from government after 1926 was possible because Labour was never close enough to any overwhelming success; its tenures of office were short-lived and precarious and it could, even when in office, be resisted and checked by constitutional means, above all through the mechanisms of parliamentary opposition and elections. The Conservatives were never forced to the desperate lengths of questioning constitutional means, as they had been in 1910–14. The Labour party too, particularly at its leadership levels, was for the most part a highly constitutionalist party wedded to (traditionally Liberal) notions of gradualist change by consent, parliamentary supremacy, electoral organisation and activity and the maximisation of social consensus. The 'moderation' which the Conservatives tended to present under Baldwin's leadership was an appropriate response to a Labour leadership and image personified until 1931 by MacDonald and Henderson. Had a 'hard left' ever been more influential and successful, whether within or outside the Labour party, then almost certainly a more significant 'hard right' would have developed in reaction against it. In the event polarisation of this kind was usually avoided and Conservative strategists could usually assume that a provocative and divisive approach from their party would be counter-productive and would alienate voters to the benefit either of Labour or of the Liberals.

The conclusion must be that the circumstances of the 1920s simply did not lend themselves to what we would characterise as right-wing extremism on a significant scale. Even the coup against the Coalition in 1922 — an outcome in which Tory resentments over Irish policy, foreign affairs problems, domestic and imperial reforms and continued high expenditure all gave an unmistakeably right-wing flavour — was not entirely a matter of the Diehard right. There was also a strong desire, not least in many of the constituency associations, for the independence of the Conservative party and for a restoration to it of full opportunities for parliamentary candidacies and government offices, a distaste for corruption over honours, and a resentment at the style and leading personalities of the Lloyd George ministry. The central roles played by the now-tamed Bonar Law and by Baldwin underlined this element of loyalism, traditionalism and constitutionalism. Coup it was, but it was scarcely a March on Rome.

One of the Tory calculations in 1922 was that the party could win a parliamentary majority in a general election by itself. (That year's election validated the judgment, though the Conservative victory was more impressive in terms of Commons seats than the share of the poll.) This preoccupation with electability was a feature of official Conservative strategy. Though the party in general was never so enthusiastic about full democracy as its rivals on the left (both the 1918 Representation Act and the 1928 'flapper' vote had Tory critics and there was some continuing distrust of the potential of democracy), the party knew that it had no choice but to work with the extended franchise and it much preferred to win majorities and hold office than to languish in minority opposition. Accordingly a prudent sensitivity to a broader national opinion than the moods of its own zealots, so far as that opinion could be gauged, was built into its responses. The central decision-makers of the party sought to assess what had traditionally been labelled 'public opinion'. This attempt was never an exact science, more a matter of interpreting a variety of auguries that included the press (an invaluable but often distorting medium), Tory backbench MPs, the party agents (often with the help of Central Office) and the local and regional associations, the prospective candidates and, of course, by-election results. The nature of this opinion, as it made itself felt upon the leadership, was liable to sudden shifts. The parliamentary Conservative party, for example, became much more right-wing when the 1929 general election reduced its numbers from 416 to 260. The members for safe seats, which were heavily concentrated in Southern England, tended to be markedly more right-wing, like their constituency associations, than those in the Midlands, the North and Scotland where so many seats were marginal and were vulnerable in a bad year. Baldwin's problems with his parliamentary party in 1929–31, when he was nearly toppled as leader, were partly a result of this shift in its ideological balance in 1929. The Tory gains of 1931 helped to restore his position. Yet even in periods of party dissension when the Diehards were off the leash, the party leaders and managers remained preoccupied not so much with the seats held safely through thick and thin but with those that would have to be won back at the next general election — and most of the crucial marginals were not like Henry Page Croft's Bournemouth. When Baldwin did eventually move in late 1930 to modify the official party line on tariffs (the 'free hand'), it was partly to save himself in a moment of danger but partly because there was now increasing evidence that opinion in many of the industrial and mixed marginals had moved towards either tariffs or at least further 'safeguarding'. Over the four general elections in 1922–9 the difference between the best and the worst performances by the Conservatives was some 160 seats. These were the marginals on which the Conservative strategists focussed, as did the rival main parties, and arguably these seats held the balance and constituted the ballast of the interwar political system. Their number and range reflected the diversity of contemporary Britain, a diversity highlighted by the dramatic disparities in economic fortunes between the regions in the period. Any party which aspired to a parliamentary majority was required to be a broad coalition of diverse industrial, class and regional interests. This requirement was always a controlling mechanism that prevented any major shift to the right by the party, just as it prevented any equivalent lurch to the left. A sudden shift of policy and image towards the Diehards might conciliate the party's own dissidents and fundamentalists, but it was likely to lose a substantial part of the centre-ground represented by the marginals and, across a great range of constituencies, by social forces like the surviving nonconformist conscience and the sizeable body of working-class Conservative sympathisers.

The class composition of the Conservative vote merits some consideration here. At the levels of leadership and personal influence the party was narrowly based in class terms (though even here it was an alliance, of landowners and of professional and business men), but it also had a considerable tail of working-class and lower middle-class support. A feature of twentieth-century Britain has been that some 30 per cent of working-class votes have usually gone to the Tories. Andrew Thorpe points out that in the seven inter-war general elections Birmingham returned 77 Unionists and only 7 Labour MPs and that most of the city's seats were dominated by a lower middle-class/skilled working-class electorate. Birmingham, with its experience of Liberal Unionism and of the Chamberlains, may have been untypical, but elsewhere there were paler versions of the same phenomenon. It is well known that the future Conservative leader Harold Macmillan sat for the depressed industrial constituency of Stockton for some of the inter-war period, but historians seem not to have bothered to ask what sorts of electors were helping to return him. The party could hardly afford to ignore this body of support among classes who were very different from the Colonel Blimps, the imperial pro-consuls, the business leaders and the professional elite who decorated the platforms of party meetings. Considerations of this kind shaped the rhetoric of Baldwin and fellow-moderates, just as they influenced the 'YMCA' group of younger Tory MPs, many of them sitting for seats where voters of this kind held the balance. Much the same could be said about the 'safeguarding' and tariff reform movements in the party. These movements were not necessarily 'right wing' in character and they often reflected concern about the fortunes of local industries and the working-class employment, as well as business profits, which depended on them. The reluctance of sections of the leadership to engage in anything like full frontal assault upon the trade unions also owed something to the recognition of the importance of the party's working-class vote, even if it represented a minority within the enfranchised working class as a whole. Here were balance-holding elements within the British political system which a party like the Conservatives could never afford to discount.

This suggests that the 'moderation' of much of the Conservative party in this period, sometimes against the grain for some of its zealots, was not merely or even mainly a matter of tradition or instinct but also of pragmatic calculation of the party's electoral interests. The answer to the failure of the extreme right to pull the Conservative party further in this direction lies less with the machinations of politicians at the centre than with the social norms and political values of certain groups, localities and regions within British society at large. One should be looking to the constituencies, in all their diversity, for the answers, not to high politics.

Despite this conclusion, one still has to ask what the respective leaders of the inter-war party offered to their followers and to the much larger numbers who voted for them without belonging to the party. Leaders, almost by definition, are not typical of their parties, but they have to be more-or-less acceptable to them, they are the image which the party presents in the public domain and they have crucial roles in the party command structures. Bonar Law, the first Tory leader from a business background, a protectionist and initially a highly truculent and combative figure, had been tamed by his experience of office during the war and in the postwar Coalition. He had remained loyal to Lloyd George until his resignation in 1921 because of ill-health. When he returned in 1922, it was not as a

Diehard himself but as a party loyalist, as a man of patriotism, decency and integrity, as a credible leader and Prime Minister and, by not being Austen Chamberlain, as someone who could hold the party together. Arguably his contribution ensured that the party did not move further to the right in the early 1920s through a continuation and intensification of the Diehard revolt. Austen Chamberlain, the shortest-lived of the party's leaders, had been too loyal to the Coalition while majority opinion among his followers was losing patience with it. He was a moderate protectionist and the most establishment-minded of the Chamberlain dynasty. As Foreign Secretary between 1924 and 1929 he sought international peace and understanding and he did much to bring about the Locarno agreement. He was almost certainly too centrist for his party, too much the respectable side of the Liberal Unionist inheritance. At the same time, though his overthrow in 1922 was revealing of the instincts of his party, it could probably have been avoided if he had been less committed to his own high-minded rectitude and less charmed personally by the coterie of talent headed by Lloyd George.

Stanley Baldwin, who led the party for fourteen years of this period, was in certain respects as centrist as Austen Chamberlain, whom he helped to depose, but more firmly committed to a sense of the party's pedigree as well as utterly uncharmed by Lloyd George. Neurotic, sensitive, an ultra-conservative rather than a Conservative Ultra, Baldwin embodied and proclaimed much of the ethos, tinged with a vague religiosity and with moral high-mindedness, of the better sort of late-Victorian family business. He was always more a moralist than an ideologue and, as a constitutionalist, he was highly distrustful of the dynamism and disruptive energy of figures like Lloyd George and Mosley. Austen Chamberlain's comment — 'I have never known ... a man who left so large a gap between the recognition that he must act and action' — summed up Baldwin's preference for normalcy, quiet and even repose over drama, excitement and heroic creativity. There was no potential for fascist-style leadership here. Indeed within the party calls for 'firmer' leadership became a coded way of criticising Baldwin. He was, however, widely recognised as an electoral asset to the Conservatives, even though in 1929 they relied too much on his personal appeal as the personification of reassurance. Baldwin was not, either in 1922 or 1931, a coalitionist by instinct, but he was a conciliator, despite his ultimate readiness to confront the miners and the TUC in 1926, and he was soon suspected by the right of his party of being too inclined to concession and compromise. Some Diehards even believed, improbably, that he was some kind of crypto-socialist.

Neville Chamberlain, a much more abrasive figure than Baldwin, came to see himself by 1930 as offering just the 'firmness' and direction that Baldwin's leadership lacked. Yet Chamberlain never called himself a Conservative — 'Unionist' was the preferred term in Chamberlainite Birmingham — and Birmingham, with its dominant lower middle/skilled working-class electorate, was always more of an influence on Neville than it was on Austen. Neville was also a more committed protectionist, not in itself a necessarily right-wing position, but he had also been a highly active legislator and social reformer during the ministry of 1924–9. Though an assertive anti-socialist who despised the Labour party for its woolly and unrealistic economic thinking and though in the 1930s the practitioner at the Treasury of the economic orthodoxy favoured by the Bank of England, Chamberlain was never a straightforward right-winger in Conservative terms. Indeed he often hankered after a political alignment broader, not narrower, than the existing Conservative party, presumably some latter-day recreation of the old Unionist alliance of his father's prime. He was never a jingoistic imperialist, never an enthusiastic rearmer (cheap government and financial prudence were more his ideals) and his policy of 'appeasement' towards the dictators when he was Prime Minister in the late 1930s would be based not on any sympathy for fascism or for his own party's ultra-right but rather on his economic orthodoxy and on his appreciation of how much British interests would suffer from any major European war.

Of the major figures of inter-war Conservatism Churchill would seem to be the most likely candidate for the extreme right. He adopted a tough line over trade union troubles in the 1920s and subsequently he emerged as the most prominent opponent of the Government of India reforms in the early 1930s when the position he represented clearly enjoyed wide support in the party. Churchill resigned from Baldwin's shadow cabinet and was excluded from the National government formed in 1931. Yet he was a former Liberal and an ex-coalitionist, he remained a convinced free-trader and he was never fully trusted by or integrated with the right wing of his new party. J.C.C. Davidson once called him 'the heaven born leader of the party — on ... only one subject, namely India'. Churchill's later opposition to 'appeasement' and his calls for determined rearmament and for firmer resistance to the dictators did not appeal to all of the Conservative right and only added to his sense of isolation within the party. But for the eventual failure of Chamberlain's foreign policy, Churchill would have remained a more marginal figure than posterity's assessment tends to assume.

At least two points emerge from this brief survey of the men who led the Conservatives from the Great War to the Second World War. The first is that their diversity and range illustrate the broad church character of the party itself. Even the official leadership did not represent a single political identity and, had the survey been extended to more of the major figures of Tory cabinets, the range would have appeared even greater. The second point is that it is not always easy to define just what the label 'right wing' should be taken to mean or to fit these figures into a single spectrum of political positions running left to right. Bonar Law, Neville Chamberlain and Churchill all prove to have had their ambiguities. Each one, at certain times, had an appeal to the Diehard right of the Conservative party, yet none of them was a straightforward right-wing figure himself. The fact that in 1940 the supposed right-winger Churchill proved to be a more accept-able Coalition premier than the apparently more 'moderate' Halifax only underlined the cross-currents of contemporary politics. Ironically one of the men who entered office for the first time in Churchill's multi-party Coali-tion was Henry Page Croft, the inveterately blimpish maverick of the Tory right who had long preached imperialism and protection, had at one point evinced sympathy for the British Union of Fascists and had, during the previous war, founded his own breakaway party to the right of Bonar Law's Conservatives. Page Croft's elevation tells us, however, little or nothing about the direction of British politics in 1940.

Then, as earlier, some of the issues did not lend themselves to a left/right categorisation. Others, like Ireland (until 1922) and Indian gov-ernment, did so. Protection, perhaps the most contentious of inter-party issues until 1931, did so less easily. Neither full tariff reform nor the more modest 'safeguarding' approach was in itself right-wing in Tory terms. While the campaign of the press lord Rothermere and of the United Empire party which he founded in 1930 with Beaverbrook could be seen in those terms, Neville Chamberlain's stance could not. Protectionists were always divided between the outright imperialists and pragmatists who saw tariffs as a matter simply of Britain's economic advantage in a difficult world. There were also free traders who, like the 4th Marquess of Salisbury, a prominent Diehard of the early 1920s, found themselves unable to co-operate easily with other right-wing elements for this reason. Foreign policy was another issue which never divided the party neatly on left/right lines and which, unlike the Indian question, served to divide the right rather than unite it. By the late 1930s the Tory right was divided between Churchill and his supporters and those elements which still sympathised with fascism. There was also a considerable body of support right across the party for Chamberlain's largely pragmatic foreign policy.

The Conservative party must be understood, therefore, as a broad church of the right, generally conservative and constitutionalist in its incli-nations and committed to its own success within an accepted electoral sys-tem, above all to the securing of parliamentary majorities and government office. It embraced a wide range of political and ideological positions and, though one consequence was constant friction, the breadth was arguably a strength to the party. Its right wing was not united or ideologically coherent, it drew relatively little support from the crucial marginal constituencies that so concerned the party's strategists and only rarely did it really threaten, rather than simply harass, the largely moderate leadership. When this did happen in 1921–2 and 1930–1, modest adjustments in party policy and in the personnel and style of leadership were capable of either satisfying or dividing the right. The danger was that a period of prolonged opposition would undermine the established leadership and strengthen its critics on the party's right, but the Conservatives' success in holding office for so much of the period prevented that. Most of the party's right usually tempered its own intransigence and settled for working to influence policy from inside the party (an aim in which it experienced mixed fortunes) rather than in challenging and splitting official Conservatism with its own breakaway parties. The strength of loyalism among party members served to encourage this prudence on the right.

The outcome of the governmental crisis of 1931, which put the Conservatives securely back into office, had restored this situation well before the British Union of Fascists appeared on the scene. Whether it would have mounted a more formidable challenge to official Conservatism in different circumstances, we can only guess. The Fascist movements of the 1920s had nibbled away at the right-wing fringes of Tory support, but had never had to be taken seriously, least of all electorally. Even in the 1920s there had been little call for a movement of intransigent confrontation with the left because the latter showed little sign of overwhelming success within the political system. The challenge of 1930–1 from Rothermere and his friends from a position well to the right of the leadership had certainly caused serious trouble, had embarrassed the party in by-elections and had forced Baldwin into various concessions. It had fed on Tory resentment of the 1929 defeat and the exile in opposition, on disenchantment with Baldwin's style of leadership and on the economic worries of Tory businessmen. As the controversy over the government of India would be, it was a sharp reminder that significant sections of the party, both within parliament and in the constituencies (some of them anyway), were to the right of their leaders and might, in other circumstances, have led in different directions. But Rothermere's challenge was collapsing even before the return of the Conservatives to office in the National government, and that government's overwhelming triumph in the 1931 general election, further handicapped the dissident right. Even if the struggle had continued beyond the spring of 1931, it would probably have led only to Baldwin's replacement by Neville Chamberlain and to a commitment to a moderate protectionist policy comparable to what later emerged from Ottawa. None of this would have entailed the triumph of a militant, confrontational and non-constitutionalist right as happened in Italy in 1922 and in Germany in 1933. By the time the BUF developed out of Mosley's earlier New party (not self-evidently right-wing in character), the circumstances which had assisted Rothermere's challenge had gone and the Tory leadership was now pulling most of the strings in a National government dependent on a large Conservative majority in the Commons. There was certainly great resentment on the right over government policy on India, which imperialists denounced as a 'retreat from empire', and Churchill was forward in exploiting the controversy. The issue added to right-wing irritation with the continuation of the National government, though the ministry's National character assisted and encouraged Baldwin and his collaborators in ignoring the outrage of the Diehards. The Government of India Act passed into law in 1935, which also saw Baldwin's return to the premiership and a National government victory at the polls which only modestly changed the parliamentary position. All told, there was no collapse or disintegration of the broad right for Mosley to exploit. The field was already occupied by a force too powerful and self-confident to be either routed or subverted.

In various respects the government had pre-empted Mosley's appeal. In the circumstances of the 1931 crisis it had itself stood for national discipline and patriotic sacrifice, it had obtained a 'doctor's mandate' to deal with financial and economic ills, and it had soon introduced a form of protection and imperial preference. The Labour opposition had been routed, the Liberals had been split. There was little for Mosley to bite on beyond the controversy over India. Much of his economic policy, where it went beyond the government's own measures, ran counter to the powerful orthodoxies respected in the City, in most political (including right-wing) circles and among most educated and influential opinion, and there was little demand for novelties that went beyond protection. The chronically depressed parts of the country, where they did not back the National candidates, were mostly loyal to the union-dominated Labour party in 1935, while the South, the Home Counties and London, areas from which the Tory right had drawn most of its following, enjoyed a degree of prosperity even during the depression years. There was little reason to throw off their electoral allegiance to the Conservatives or to choke on the leadership provided by Baldwin and Chamberlain, even though there was Tory resentment that MacDonald survived as premier until 1935 and that a National (rather than a fully Conservative) government continued. There was some initial sympathy among Tories for the BUF and a degree of curiosity about its nature and prospects, but such sympathy was soon to be alienated. The strain of direct action and violence in fascism went well beyond the 'firmness' and 'leadership' Tories had demanded from their own front bench and could be seen as potentially destabilising, socially disruptive and harmful to civil order. It turned many sympathisers against the BUF, including a number of Tory MPs who had been inquisitive enough to attend Mosley's Olympia rally of 1934 and elements in the police who now became increasingly hostile to Fascist or Fascist-provoked street disturbances. All this added to the sense that the BUF, which was so obviously imitative of continental models, was both alien and unconstitutional. When disorder escalated, the government was able to rush a Public Order Act with a clear anti-Fascist purpose into law in 1936 without serious dissent from its own supporters. Just as the economic panaceas offered by Mosley ran up against the orthodoxies of the Tory right, so his constitutional radicalism affronted Conservatives wedded to the established parliamentary constitution. And why should the conservative right want to abandon a constitution within which it was succeeding so well? Though modest numbers on the Conservative right remained soft on fascism, particularly in the European context where they saw it as a barrier to advancing communism, in domestic politics the BUF had put itself beyond the Tory pale by 1936. Its electoral irrelevance had been emphasised by the 1935 general election. It had become a sideshow to the main preoccupations of British domestic politics and to the central electoral confrontation between the Conservatives and Labour in a now virtually two-party system. Not even the Spanish Civil War, which encouraged a sense of left/right polarisation in British politics, altered that reality.

Baldwin and Chamberlain were good foils to what Mosley offered. Baldwin appeared as the personification of the stability and reassurance which much national opinion desired. Chamberlain, a more constructive, sharp-edged and modernising politician and a talented administrator, gave a sense of direction and decisiveness to government in the years after 1931. His decisiveness and abrasiveness with the Labour opposition provided the 'firmness' which many Tories felt Baldwin lacked. Between them they helped their party to continue to dominate the centre-right of national politics. The BUF could never hope to challenge the Conservatives directly and never enjoyed the opportunities which a fragmentation of the broad right might have given them. The evident divisions on the right over policy towards the dictators after 1936 only confirmed the difficulties that faced the separatist right.

This outcome was much more than the influence of two formidable politicians. It followed from the circumstances of the inter-war period as a whole and from the position the Conservative party occupied within it.

Neither the political nation in general nor the Conservative party itself suffered any prolonged sense of failure of the kind the Tories had experienced before 1914. Though there were two moments when the Diehard element within the party and other right-wing elements seemed to pose a serious threat to what the party leadership represented, the possibilities never had the chance to develop further and the centre-right of British politics never disintegrated. The broad right remained largely satisfied with the Conservative party while it held office for so much of the time, while it continued to command such a considerable body of support across most of the nation's constituencies and while the political left could never pose a serious threat to the interests of major property and privilege. Right-wing extremism 'failed', not simply from failings of its own, but because circumstances never provided it with a role centre-stage.

The Failure of British Fascism 1932-40

BY RICHARD THURLOW

The literature on British fascism has shown differences of interpretation about its failure to make a significant political impact in the inter-war years. No-one wastes any time in explaining why such quixotic and eccentric movements as the British Fascisti in the 1920s and the Imperial Fascist League in the 1930s were minute elements on the political fringe. The British Union of Fascists (BUF) however presents a more serious problem; its activities undoubtedly caused both hostile reactions to it in society, and caused significant problems for the authorities in the 1930s. In general terms, existing interpretations have highlighted four main areas where a long catalogue of negative reasons for fascism's failure in Britain have been adduced. These relate to how it misconceived the nature of the crisis in British society in the inter-war period; why it was alien to British political culture; the personnel, organisation and ideological weaknesses of the BUF; and both state management and the hostility of the left as factors in minimising its political impact. Whilst the main interpretations would accept that all these explanations were important there is considerable difference as to their relative significance. Brewer and Lewis have emphasised the first, Benewick, Skidelsky, Nicholas Mosley and Holmes the second, Lebzelter and Anderson the fourth, and Thurlow the third and fourth of these categories of explanation in published material, and other scholars such as Rawnsley have produced interpretations in unpublished work providing new insights on several of these factors, particularly the third.[1] However, even where there

---

[1] See Further Reading for details.

is agreement on the importance of relevant factors, there is disagreement on the reasons why this should be so as the differences, for example, between Brewer's and Lewis's approach and Benewick's and Skidelsky's show. The purpose of this paper, however, is not so much to award brownie points with regard to the competing views, but to argue that the problem needs to be re-cast in the light of new material and to suggest that more attention needs to be given to the role of the authorities in the explanation of the failure of British fascism.

The release of four separate batches of most of the surviving Home Office material on British fascism between 1932 and 1940 and the availability of other new sources has given us much new information about the role of state management and the nature of political opposition to British fascism. In particular it has enabled a study of why, despite its obvious political failure and lack of impact, the authorities still found it necessary to close down British fascism in 1940 and to outlaw the BUF. What most books on British fascism have in common is that the cut-off date for study is 1939 rather than 1940. This is unfortunate because the events of 1940, and the authorities' reaction to them, tell us much about the British state's attitude towards political extremism in general and the limits of tolerance in a liberal society. With this in mind this essay will now examine the four general categories of explanation.

The role of 'crisis' (Brewer) or 'trauma' (Lewis) and the BUF's misconception of its nature in Britain in the 1930s is seen as a societal explanation for the failure of British fascism. Whether one believes that Mosley had a neo-Marxian view of the British economy in the 1930s or a Spenglerean interpretation of the slow decline of western civilisation, and if it was part of a long-run or immediate crisis, he was undoubtedly wrong in his estimation of its impact. Mosley appeared to believe that the persistence of high levels of unemployment since 1920, with its inexorable rise to 3 million by 1933, needed a revolution based on the authoritarian leadership of the new man of fascism to be resolved. This derived from a belief that unemployment leads to political radicalism, that only fascism with its activism and dynamism and its pragmatic programme to cure unemployment, outlined in *The Greater Britain*, could solve the problem. There were several fallacies in this argument. Firstly unemployment in the inter-war period was particularly a regional and structural problem of the economy with much higher rates north and west of the Humber-Severn line than south and east of it. After the end (July 1934) of the 'Rothermere period' of *Daily Mail* support, all the evidence suggests that the main centres of British fascism were south and east of the Humber-Severn line. Indeed, apart from the Cotton Campaign in Lancashire in 1934–5 there is little evidence that the

BUF ever made much impact in the areas of high unemployment such as Central Scotland, North East England or South Wales. Indeed all these areas were centres of militant resistance to attempted Fascist incursions. Secondly, insofar as the unemployed were concerned with politics, they were much more likely to respond to the reformist policies of most trade unions and the Labour party than radical solutions. What small proportion of the unemployed were politically radicalised became so under Communist party and National Unemployed Workers' Movement auspices rather than Fascist. As a result most of the unemployed were either hostile or apathetic to Mosley and the BUF. Thirdly, as Harry Harmer has shown, the NUWM, which was basically a Communist party front organisation, only made headway amongst the unemployed when it could be shown that it was useful in the reformist activity of support at referees' tribunals for benefit payments.[2] Although the BUF tried to be active in such areas too, it made little impact amongst the unemployed. For a revolutionary party whose chief *raison d'être* was to solve the unemployment problem the BUF was viewed negatively by those who failed to obtain work.

Indeed Mosley appeared not only to lack an appeal to most of the unemployed but to display a singular lack of realism about the economy's problems. By arguing that democracy and the 'old gangs' could not solve Britain's economic and political problems in the 1930s he was patently unable to explain the economic recovery after 1931. The abandonment of the gold standard in 1931, low interest rates, mild reflation and empire preference after 1932 helped produce a small stimulus to the British economy which was also encouraged by the increase in real wages for those in work in the 1930s.[3] Although much of this was unintentional, the National government showed that although it was little more than the Conservative party in disguise, nevertheless economic recovery did not need the draconian authoritarian solution of Mosley to resolve Britain's ills. Even though recovery was far from uniform, the vast majority preferred Britain's slow economic decline to the utopian programmes of political extremists of the left and right. Mosley was to make as little impact amongst those in work as with the unemployed in the 1930s.

This raises the question: to whom did Mosley appeal in the 1930s? Mosley failed because he only attracted marginal elements from several so-

---

[2] H.J.P. Harmer, 'The National Unemployed Workers' Movement in Britain 1921-39: failure and success', unpubd. London Univ. Ph.D. thesis, 1987, pp. 156–84; cf. R. Croucher, *We Refuse to Starve in Silence* (1987), pp. 113–17.

[3] S. Pollard, *The Development of the British Economy* (1969), pp. 92–174; B. Alford, *Depression and Recovery* (1972); D.H. Aldcroft, *The Inter War Economy* (1973).

cial groups into the BUF. Gerry Webber has suggested Mosley's main appeal was to discontented Conservatives, particularly during the Rothermere period (January–July 1934) and in the heyday of appeasement (1938–9). He calculated, using chief constables' returns from MI5 reports and Special Branch material, that membership rose from 17,000 in February 1934 to a peak of 50,000 in July 1934, a collapse to 5,000 in October 1935, a slow recovery to 10,000 in March 1936, 15,500 in November 1936, 16,500 in December 1938 and 22,500 in September 1939.[4] Although these figures in the later 1930s mirrored the growth of the Communist party, the levels were dependent on counting passive supporters as well as active members. It also appears that the spatial distribution of members was somewhat patchy. Apart from a few outposts of fascism in South Wales, Scotland and Ulster, the BUF was misnamed. The BUF was predominantly an English movement with its main area of strength in London and the South East although there was sizeable support in Manchester, Liverpool and Leeds in 1934. In the Rothermere period the movement appealed to a broader spectrum which cut across social class divisions. With rapid decline the focus of recruitment shifted to the North West, and between 1935 and 1938 to the anti-semitic campaign in the East End of London. In the later 1930s the gradual shift towards recruiting more middle-class, elderly and right-wing members was accentuated by the peace campaign, mainly in South and East England.

The high turnover of membership, the instability and rootlessness of the movement, and its fluctuating fortunes in different areas tend to suggest that the BUF attracted the alienated, some idealists and those with chips on their shoulders. Special Branch noted its attraction to criminal elements and its generally disreputable nature particularly in the East End of London. In the few areas where it did stand in elections, it did uniformly badly outside its stronghold of the East End of London where it gained 22 per cent of the vote in Bethnal Green in 1937. In the three parliamentary seats it stood for in 1939–40 it gained 1 per cent, 1 per cent and 2 per cent in the three by-elections, usually standing against the incumbent party nominee only.

David Lewis's argument that the BUF, like other European fascist movements, was basically centrist in its appeal as well as its ideology, has to be viewed critically, unless centrism is to be interpreted as a meaningless broad class spectrum. Lewis's interesting case, based on a selective survey of comparative fascist movements, ignores the fact that the most interesting

---
[4] G. Webber, 'Patterns of membership and support for the British Union of Fascists', *Journal of Contemporary History*, 19 (1984), pp. 575-606.

empirical surveys of German nazism suggest that its main source of support was in rural Protestant areas and amongst the traditional right in urban centres, that fascism was a surrogate form of leftism in an environment where the left had been outlawed in eastern Europe, and that in Italy, because of the fear of communism, fascism appealed to a broad spectrum which included the urban middle class, landowners and some peasants.[5]

Lewis's sophisticated neo-Marxist interpretation suggests correctly that Britain's political system did not undergo the same degree of 'trauma' as Italy and Germany in the inter-war period and that therefore the liberal 'centre' accepted the milder form of leadership of the National government rather than Mosley's extremism. Although Lewis's stimulating comparisons are interesting, he is surely wrong to imply that if conditions had not improved in Britain in the 1930s Mosley would have been seen as a saviour rather than the political pariah he became. Although Mosley brought his message to nearly the centre of the Establishment in the social activities of the January Club in 1934, there is little evidence that he made many converts to the Fascist cause even at the peak of Conservative unrest against the National government in 1934. Mosley attracted adherents from both the left and the right, as well as a large majority who had no previous experience of conventional politics, but the 'third way' in British society cut little ice. Neither public opinion nor the Establishment were to take any notice of the increasingly isolated figure of Mosley and the British Union of Fascists, particularly as he became increasingly associated with negative associations, most notably anti-semitism, political violence and unconditional support for the dictators.

Finally it is ironic to note that the 'lack of a crisis' interpretation fails to assess the impact of the events of 1939–40, which eventually led to the closing down of British fascism. When a real crisis emerged with the 'fifth column' and invasion scares of 1940 the state moved quickly to destroy British fascism, despite the lack of incriminating evidence. This suggests that state management of British fascism played a crucial behind the scenes role in helping account for its failure, or at least in monitoring and assisting its demise. This complex story, however, will be examined later.

The second argument which has been used to explain fascism's failure in Britain was that it was alien to Britain's political culture. This argument had several strands including the charge that the BUF was too closely modelled on foreign derivatives, that it was in some way controlled by these foreign powers, that it was inherently dictatorial and hierarchical

---

[5] R. Hamilton, *Who Voted For Hitler?* (Guildford, 1982); D. Muhlberger (ed.), *The Social Basis of European Fascism* (1987), pp. 1–39, 281–319.

and was antithetical to the liberal British parliamentary political tradition, and that its activities increasingly became involved with the 'low politics' of street corner society with its dubious involvement with political violence and anti-semitism. There was also the position of Oswald Mosley to consider; the politician, who had married Lord Curzon's daughter, and whose connections and talents hinted at a sparkling career at the centre of British politics, yet who had, in the titles of Nicholas Mosley's books on his relationship with his father, bucked *The Rules of the Game* and gone *Beyond the Pale*.

Whilst Mosley and the BUF had rational answers to all these arguments, the point is that public opinion viewed the BUF in an increasingly suspicious and negative light in the 1930s, and came to blame the BUF for the major share in the public order problems which resulted from its activities. The history of British politics is littered with the debris of 'third force' political parties trying to break the mould of the political system. Although the Labour party had split in 1931 with the formation of the National government, and had been reduced to a rump of 46 seats in the House of Commons, neither Mosley's New party nor later the BUF were to make any inroads into Labour's place as the official opposition. As the Liberals, the Social Democratic party and the Social and Liberal Democrats have recently experienced, breaking the mould requires a degree of luck, talent, resources, support and political credibility which is extremely difficult to manufacture and which has only been achieved by the Labour party in the twentieth century, following the special circumstances of the split in the Liberal party in 1916. As well as these difficulties Mosley and the BUF were further hindered by their opposition to the parliamentary system itself in a situation where the National government was presiding over a slow but sustained recovery of the British economy in the 1930s. In this situation the demand for a replacement of the traditions of parliamentary government by the Corporate State, and for a 'revolution' in British government fell on deaf ears. Public opinion viewed the Fascists, like the Communists, as extremists and part of the political fringe.

British fascism suffered also from its close identification with the excesses of Italian fascism and German nazism in the public mind. In spite of BUF propaganda that its programme and organisation sprang entirely from British traditions, its unfortunate similarities with aspects of foreign movements were obvious to all. The most visible sign of this was the uniform until it was banned by the Public Order Act of 1936. The Blackshirt reminded the public of Mussolini's Italy and the jackboots of Hitler's Germany. Attempts to explain the flash in the circle as an ancient British symbol deriving from the occupation of the British Isles by Ancient Rome were laughable. Although political violence in the 1930s was never to approach the level it did in Italy in the early 1920s, or the anti-semitic campaign with the excesses of nazi Germany, respectable opinion dropped Mosley after the Olympia fiasco in 1934. The activities of the fascist states also rebounded negatively on the BUF even though they had no share in them. The political murders and illegality of the Night of the Long Knives on 30 June 1934 was a factor in leading Rothermere to end his support for the BUF in the *Daily Mail*. The hostile response of public opinion to Mussolini's invasion of Abyssinia in 1935, the material and military help given by the dictators to Franco in the Spanish Civil War and the invasion of rump Czechoslovakia in March 1939 all produced hostile public reactions to the BUF.

What made matters worse for Mosley was the fact that, despite the line that fascism derived from separate national traditions in different countries, he at no stage was critical of any of the dictators' actions. For example he responded to Mussolini's invasion of Abyssinia with the 'Mind Britain's Business' campaign in 1935. This raised natural suspicions that Mosley, at the very least, had more than ideological ties with the dictators. We now know that Mussolini provided at least £40,000 to BUF coffers in 1933–4 and possibly much more, thanks to the discovery of Count Grandi's correspondence. (Grandi was the Italian ambassador in London at this period.)[6] Although Hitler provided Mosley with no money, the fact that he was prepared to build Mosley a radio transmitter to help him corner the market in private radio shows that Mosley stood to gain from the maintenance of peace in Europe. Neither of these facts was known at the time; but public opinion was increasingly suspicious of a man and a movement who had nothing critical to say about fascist Italy or nazi Germany, particularly in the light of the massive financial outlay involved in the leasing of 'Black House' (Whitelands teacher training college in Chelsea) and the employment of 350 full-time administrators paid at union rates in 1934. Indeed Mosley seemed to envisage a carve-up of the world's resources by the future fascist powers of Britain, Italy and Germany in an article in *Fascist Quarterly* in 1936.[7] The later image of Mosley as an 'absurd strutting megalomaniac' appears to have its roots in such connections.

The Corporate State, which Lewis sees as the lynchpin of Mosley's ideas in the 1930s, was also associated in the public's mind with an alien political tradition. Although the Mond-Turner agreements of 1928 were seen by some as the harbinger of improved industrial relations, compulsory

---

[6] D. Irving, *Focal Point*, 30 Oct. 1981; N. Mosley, *Beyond the Pale* (1983), pp. 30–4.

[7] O. Mosley, 'The world alternative', *Fascist Quarterly* 2, 3 (1936).

arbitration and an era of class harmony in industry following the failure of
the General Strike, most workers viewed the Corporate State with suspicion
as a result of Mussolini's blatant emasculation of the Italian working class
and Hitler's disregard of the concept. The Corporate State was a figleaf to
mask capitalist exploitation of the workers as far as the left was concerned
and a further reason why British fascism should be opposed.

The other alien political tradition with which the BUF became indeli-
bly associated in the public mind was anti-semitism. Although there had
been a tradition of political anti-semitism in the East End of London dating
from the activities of the British Brothers League in the Edwardian era,[8]
public opinion interpreted the BUF campaign as a last desperate throw of
the dice of a declining movement which was deliberately trying to imitate
nazi success with the issue. The anti-semitic campaign between 1935 and
1938 has to be seen as part of a strategy whereby the BUF adopted populist
tactics to use local grievances to help drum up support for the movement
after the failure of the national campaign. This tactic was locally very successful in three areas of the East End but was highly counter-productive
elsewhere. Although chauvinist and ethnocentric resentment of successful minorities had always been a social problem, political anti-semitism
offended the tolerant and ethical beliefs of the dominant liberal political
culture. Although other groups and political parties were critical of some
aspects of Jewish behaviour patterns in the East End of London, overt anti-
semitism together with the growth of subterranean violence and other forms
of illegal activity was classed as unacceptable behaviour by most people.
Only in the East End was the BUF to be a political force after 1935.

Finally fascism had prospered in Europe where there had been a credible threat of communist revolution. This had never been the case in Britain
despite the alarm felt by Tory ministers in the period of industrial unrest
following the First World War.[9] The defeat of the threatened use of the
Triple Alliance in 1921 and of the General Strike in 1926 showed that the
authorities had managed to contain neo-syndicalist threats. Similarly the
failure of the Communist party in the 1920s made Mosley's claim that fascism was needed to contain 'red terrorism' a hollow one. The authorities
perceived the BUF as an extremist organisation, not as an ally in the fight
against Communist subversion. Somewhat ironically MI5 perceived that
extremism grew where law and order was threatened and that the growth
of the two political extremes fed off one another. However they also implied
that Mosley's potential appeal quickly disintegrated. Those who joined the

---

[8] C. Holmes, *Anti-Semitism in British Society, 1876-1939* (1979), pp. 89–97.
[9] R.K. Middlemas (ed.), T. Jones, *Whitehall Diary* (3 vols., 1969), I:99–103.

BUF because they thought he was defending free speech against Communist attacks became rapidly disillusioned with the military discipline and hierarchical structure of the organisation.

The internal weaknesses of the BUF were the third factor explaining why it made so little impact. The problems with the BUF started with Mosley himself. These related both to blatant contradictions between ideas and his leadership position and his delegation of the administrative functions of the movement. Mosley's credibility was questioned because his personality made it difficult for him to work through political compromise. Mosley believed that the method of synthesis could harmonise opposing ideas at a higher level of political reality. However Mosley's political odyssey showed he found the art of political compromise difficult in the real world. His inability to harmonise opposing views to his led him to leave both the Conservative and Labour parties in 1923 and 1931 and his move to fascism lost him much of his left-wing support. His fascist career led to constant arguments with many leaving the movement. As a result, while influential interest was attracted by Mosley's pragmatic radicalism this drawback meant Mosley only retained consistent support from inexperienced political mavericks. Mosley, despite his theoretical belief in synthesis, appeared unable to accept criticism of his ideas and had to operate in an autocratic fashion where he brought the tablets down from the mountain to his adoring supporters. This lack of criticism led to an increasingly unrealistic fascist doctrine based on utopian assumptions. His plans for autarkic empire development for example, with Britain providing the manufactured goods and the empire the primary products, ignored the fact that such policies would be militantly opposed by the dominions, who at the Ottawa conference in 1932 were principally concerned with protecting their own industrial sectors. It is not surprising that the BUF made no impact in the British Empire.

If Mosley's increasingly unrealistic views and his inability to compromise were a drawback for the BUF then his delegation of all responsibility for the administration and organisation of the BUF was a calamity. A leading nazi agent, Colin Ross, reputedly reported to Hitler that the BUF had a fine leader but absolutely no organisation.[10] The truth of that was highlighted by the 1935 general election which the BUF boycotted using the slogan 'Fascism next time'. Mosley argued that he devoted his energies to formulating the programme of the BUF and to public speaking. This was understandable given that Mosley was without peer as a public speaker in twentieth century British politics. However, although Mosley's meetings

---

[10] P[ublic] R[ecord] O[ffice]: HO 144/21060/55.

undoubtedly led to recruitment, the administrative and financial structure of the movement, which Mosley left to others, left much to be desired. Although Major-General J.F.C. Fuller helped reorganise the movement on military lines in 1936, the changing administrative structure occasioned by financial cutbacks in the later 1930s caused organisational problems. Mosley proved less than decisive in dealing with factional divisions in the movement until he was forced to do so by financial necessity in 1937. Mosley sided with the administrative clique led by Neil Francis-Hawkins against the fascist propagandists, William Joyce, John Beckett and A.K. Chesterton, who all left the movement. However, although Mosley got rid of his most notorious members, the BUF remained anti-semitic and was forever to be smeared by bringing to public attention the anti-semitic diatribes and later treason of William Joyce.

If the administration and organisation of the BUF was a calamity then its finance was a disaster. Mosley argued that he delegated financial aspects of the movement to others so he could concentrate on ideas and public speaking. A more sceptical interpretation would suggest that Mosley wished to try to mask the real sources of his movement's finance and leave him with the excuse that he knew nothing of its source. The fact that the accountants heavily criticised the books of the BUF between 1933 and 1937 and that Special Branch discovered a secret bank account through which £224,000 in foreign currency was laundered into BUF funds between 1933 and 1937 suggests a cover-up. Mosley argued before the Advisory Commission on Internment in 1940 that this money was provided by British entrepreneurs wishing to contribute to BUF funds.[11] It is true that Mosley received £80,000 from motor car and aeroplane entrepreneurs in the New party in 1931 and no doubt some of this may have continued in the BUF. However the fact that he received money from Mussolini suggests there were obvious reasons for his secretive behaviour. Mosley himself alleged he poured £100,000 down the political drain of British fascism in the 1930s and the audited accounts show he paid £24,000 into them from his own funds in 1938–9.

In addition, the failure of Mosley to exert tight financial control until the later 1930s was nearly disastrous. Special Branch reported that one of the reasons why Robert Forgan resigned from the deputy leadership of the BUF was because of lax financial administration.[12] They also suggested that there was much petty corruption and siphoning off of BUF funds in the middle 1930s by the more light-fingered members. This has been confirmed

---

[11] PRO: HO 283/14/8.
[12] PRO: HO 144/20145/222–5.

by Stuart Rawnsley's study of fascism in Lancashire. While corruption was a problem in the early 1930s, the effects of destabilising financial cutbacks in the later 1930s when the foreign currency dried up led to increasing friction and administrative restructuring within the movement. This involved the reduction of the payroll from 350 to 50 between 1936 and 1939.[13] In 1937 alone there was a 70 per cent cut in expenditure. No doubt the BUF became a leaner, fitter organisation but despite the fact that many sacked officials remained in a voluntary capacity such deep cuts affected the ability of the administrative centre to control the regions. In spite of the dedication of the remaining administrators and volunteers these problems undoubtedly hindered the recovery of the BUF in the later 1930s.

The fourth factor, that of opposition to British fascism both by the state and the political left is an area which has not been fully researched, yet the evidence now available suggests it was very significant. Somewhat ironically the state viewed the anti-Fascist activities of the left as stimulating political extremism in general and were particularly concerned about the increase in anti-semitism and the possible alliance between Communists and Fascists based on criticism of Jewish behaviour. This of course was a delusion even in the period of the Nazi-Soviet Pact (1939–41). The left, or at least the Communist party and its allies, saw the government as being in league with the Fascists. Certainly the Communist party gained steadily in strength through the 1930s from 3,000 to 17,000 members, and one of its most successful areas was the East End of London. However, opposition to Mosley and the Battle of Cable Street in 1936 were only minor factors in the recovery of the Communist party in the 1930s; emphasis on trades unions, grassroots political activism in tenant associations and other organisations, and recruitment for the International Brigade and support for the Republicans in Spain were more important factors in this growth. Indeed there is evidence that the leadership of the Communist party, like that of the Labour party, wished to ignore the activities of the BUF as far as possible and were only forced to accept the leadership of an anti-Mosley campaign by the spontaneous hostility shown to the BUF by many political activists in the London Labour movement.[14] What was undoubtedly the case, however, was that Communist and Jewish activist protest against the BUF led to violence and public order problems which public opinion chiefly blamed the Fascists for creating.

Marxists, although no longer holding the Stalinist 'twin brother' interpretation or the theoretical gyrations of the Nazi-Soviet Pact period of

---

[13] R. Thurlow, *Fascism in Britain: a history, 1918–85* (Oxford, 1987), p. 134.

[14] J. Jacobs, *Out of the Ghetto* (1978), pp. 222–58.

1939–41, still base their interpretation of fascism on the 'united front' policies of the later 1930s. Although this is much more defensible than the logical absurdities of the other Stalinist interpretations it still over-simplifies
the role of the state and its attitude towards political extremism. This is
true of both contemporary political activism against neo-fascism and the
best interpretations of the 1930s by those influenced by the Marxist tradition like David Lewis.[15]

Marxist-Leninist theories of revolution argue that economic crisis, class
consciousness, the role of the vanguard party and splits in the ruling class
are all necessary ingredients. Gramscian ideas of the hegemony of liberal
political values and the incorporation of the working class under reformist
influence suggest an explanation of why Marxist ideas had such little impact
in Britain. While the Communists were obviously more successful than the
BUF in recruiting the working class, neither made any but sporadic and
marginal impact on the reformist traditions of British society in the inter-
war period. With the recovery of the British economy in the 1930s and the
Comintern obviously pulling most of the strings behind the oscillations in
Communist party policy, the independent vanguard role of the CP leadership was obviously compromised. The divisions in the Establishnment
were more interesting, however. Although there was complete agreement
in maintaining the nature of the political system from across the parliamentary spectrum there was a considerable disagreement between politicians
and amongst the various agencies of state as to how both fascism and communism should be managed. Policy altered with relation to the use of the
law to minimise the threat posed by political extremism at various times.
Communist leaders were imprisoned in 1925 and their literature banned
in 1940, for example. However in general measures were taken, against
both Fascists and Communists, only as a result of attempts to get as much
consensus as possible across the parliamentary spectrum. In this the con-
stantly changing influences and pressures on politicians and the dominance
of the liberal political tradition, particularly in the Home Office, were to
be of crucial significance.

It was the independence of the various agencies of state and the limited degree of government influence on the police, the judiciary and the
security services which were most important with regard to the authorities'
management of British fascism. The structure of legislation with regard to
fundamental civil liberties and freedom of opinion is based on the common
law and the independence of the various agencies of state. These can be
regulated by administrative response with relation to specific problems as

---

[15] D. Lewis, *Illusions of Grandeur* (Manchester, 1987), pp. 257–68.

they arise, but the basic requirement is to give the authorities as much freedom of manoeuvre as possible and not to be hampered by specific case-law.
Hence the response of the state to political extremism in the inter-war years
was to move slowly and with the maximum degree of consensus within the
Establishment and across the parliamentary spectrum. Only when public
order was threatened, as in 1936 after the Battle of Cable Street, or the
system faced external threats, as in 1940, did the state move to restrict the
civil liberties of those whom it considered to be political extremists. Otherwise the state's policy was one of political surveillance, monitoring the
activities of such groups and taking other administrative action in response
to events.

The attitude of the state towards British fascism was worked out at
a conference called at the Home Office on 23 November 1933 to discuss
the BUF. Attended by Home Office officials, the Metropolitan Police Commissioner, Lord Trenchard, MI5 officers and a representative from Special
Branch, the conference decided not to ban uniforms but for Special Branch
to collect information on fascism in Britain and for MI5 to evaluate this
and other sources.[16] It was this material which was to provide the essential
background to the management by the state of British fascism in the 1930s
and which shows that covert activity was at least as responsible for policy
as overt behaviour by the Fascists or the state.

In terms of the political Establishment, Mosley and the BUF were seen
as political mavericks who posed public order problems. A few right-wing
Conservatives saw the BUF as a Diehard ally in the anti-Communist crusade but in general most Tories saw Mosley as a disreputable figure, 'a
cad and a wrong 'un', as Baldwin allegedly put it.[17] For most Conservatives not only was Mosley suspect as he did not play the party game,
but his cavalier lifestyle offended against the morality of the narrow Nonconformist puritan conscience which so dominated inter-war politics. The
Labour party saw Mosley as a traitor, who not only supported what they
considered an immoral political creed, which in Italy and Germany had
been responsible for the murder and imprisonment of trade unionists and
socialists, but who had tried to split the Labour party when the New party
was formed. The Liberals too saw Mosley as suspect despite Lloyd George's
admiration of his dynamism. However, although Herbert Morrison claimed
in a deputation to the Home Secretary, Sir John Simon, in 1936 that the
local political parties in the East End wished to ban the Fascists in the
aftermath of Cable Street, the general response of the political parties was

---

[16] PRO: HO 45/25386/54–9.
[17] Middlemas (ed.), *Whitehall Diary*, II:195.

that surveillance of the Fascists should be continued and that negative or no publicity of the Fascists should be encouraged. Hence the banning or discouragement of the newsreels from filming extremist demonstrations was intimated. After Rothermere dropped the Fascists in July 1934, newspaper editors were advised to ignore the BUF. It was suggested to the BBC that it should not become a platform for advertising extremist views, and Mosley was effectively prevented from the use of the media between 1935 and 1968. Local authorities increasingly banned the use of council property for Fascist meetings. The state thought the best means of shunting Mosley into the political sidings was to ignore him. The CP and Jewish activists thought otherwise and those found guilty of breaking the law or creating disturbances were to be treated more harshly than the Fascists.

The politician with the most responsibility for the management of British fascism in the 1930s was the Home Secretary. In the period when fascism was a problem between 1933 and 1940 there were four Home Secretaries, Sir John Gilmour, Sir John Simon, Sir Samuel Hoare and Sir John Anderson. They all received advice from the law officers, the permanent civil servants in the Home Office, the Metropolitan Police Commissioner and MI5. All were to play key roles and the need for consensus meant that more active state intervention was rare. Thus public order legislation was dropped in 1932 after the NUWM demonstration because the Attorney General, Sir Thomas Inskip, thought that restrictions on processions and demonstrations would infringe civil liberties. In 1934 attempts to ban uniforms foundered on political disagreements, the improvement of public order after Olympia and the increasing hostility of the permanent Home Office officials to Lord Trenchard, the Metropolitan Police Commissioner. The passing of the Public Order Act followed pressure from Sir Philip Game, who argued he needed more powers to ban processions to prevent a recurrence of the Battle of Cable Street, and there were continuing attempts by Home Office officials to limit its application after 1937. Far from representing a coherent assault on civil liberties, as the Council for Civil Liberties contended, the Public Order Act and its implementation arose from a series of compromises reflecting different viewpoints.

Of these the attitudes of the Metropolitan Police Commissioners, Lord Trenchard (1931–5) and Sir Philip Game (1935–46) were to be most important. Trenchard, the founder of the RAF, pushed through a series of controversial police reforms with the support of Sir John Gilmour, the Home Secretary.[18] His authoritarian style, and no doubt the close connections Mosley had with the RAF led the Communists to argue that he protected

---

[18] A. Boyle, *Trenchard* (1962), pp. 620–1.

the BUF from hostile demonstrations. Nothing could be further from the truth. Trenchard wished to ban the Fascists because of the public order problems they presented and he particularly wanted to outlaw the wearing of political uniforms. He did not want uniformed stewarding of meetings outside police control, neither did he want the police to be seen as protecting Fascists.

Sir Philip Game, who was Trenchard's leading administrator in the RAF, wanted to ban political anti-semitism and failing that to restrict the right of Fascists to march in the East End of London. He had particular influence over Sir Samuel Hoare, who was one of Trenchard's keenest political supporters in the inter-service battle of the 1920s. Game, however, was found to be much more accommodating than his predecessor by the Home Office officials. Nevertheless, Hoare supported the continued implementation of the ban, under section 3.3 of the Public Order Act, of processions in the East End of London against the advice of his officials and in support of Game during 1938.[19]

Thus as far as official police attitudes were concerned they were far from being pro-Fascist as the Communists contended. Although the Public Order Act was as much concerned with regulating anti-Fascist protest as with controlling the Fascists it was obvious that the legislation outlawing political uniforms had the Blackshirts particularly in mind. At the street level, however, the attitudes and operational problems of individual policemen meant that the even-handed approach was difficult to implement. 'H' Division in Bethnal Green was particularly notorious for policemen treating anti-Fascist protestors more harshly than the Fascists. This was because the Fascists obeyed all police instructions whilst the Communists protested infringement of their civil liberties. Although some policemen were cautioned or disciplined for not arresting blatantly abusive anti-semitic speakers, Game was forced to admit that the tactics of the Fascist speakers kept most of them within the law and that this was difficult to enforce. Magistrates too dispensed summary jurisdiction more harshly with regard to anti-Fascist demonstrators than with the Fascists. The Public Order Act, although open to criticism on civil liberties grounds, however, helped control the situation in the East End prior to the Second World War. The banning of processions after April 1937 in the East End of London helped the authorities to control tension in the area even if sporadic violence and anti-semitic incidents continued unabated.

If the overt actions of the state dominated the authorities' attitude towards the Fascists in the 1930s, then the covert activities of the security

---

[19] PRO: HO 144/21087/268.

services were of particular importance in 1939–40. What destroyed whatever small credibility the BUF had was the accusation that they could be seen as an incipient 'fifth column' in any war against the nazis. The contradiction between the super-nationalist ideology of the BUF and uncritical support of the dictators in the later 1930s increased suspicion even if the BUF maintained there was no clash of vital interests. During the so-called 'phoney war' period there was an increasing battle over national security between the liberal political traditions of the Home Office and the increasingly restrictionist MI5 which with the collapse of the Western Front in April and May 1940 led to a change of policy, the effective suspension of habeas corpus, and the internment of aliens and many Fascists.

In 1939 the Home Secretary and Minister for Home Security was Sir John Anderson. This position was one of the peaks of his distinguished career. He had been a career civil servant who had been Permanent Secretary at the Home Office between 1922 and 1932. He had been responsible during his career for overseeing security policy in Ireland during the troubles, the preparations against the General Strike and combating terrorism in Bengal. The evidence suggests that although at several points he found it necessary for administrative reasons to introduce or implement measures which restricted civil liberties he did so only with reluctance. Thus he viewed the introduction of Emergency Powers in August 1939, and of the various Defence Regulations which followed it, as giving him powers to act if necessary and the authorities moved very cautiously over internment before March 1940. In general terms he was the personification of the Home Office tradition that civil liberties should be restricted as little as possible and only then as a result of urgent administrative necessity. In May 1940 he resisted the internment of both aliens and Fascists until the pressure of events forced him to accept their necessity.[20]

Against this the significant expansion of MI5 during 1939 led to increasing influence. Until the outbreak of war the Communists rather than the Fascists had been the main extremist group that was of concern to the authorities. Indeed the military and empire connections of many MI5 officers led to some sympathy with the discipline of the BUF. Maxwell Knight, head of B5b, the agent-running section, had reputedly been a research officer in the British Fascists during the 1920s. During the 1930s the BUF's growth in 1934 had been viewed with concern but from 1935 onwards it was seen as a minor public order irritant. From the outbreak of war it was viewed with increasing paranoia. Agents' reports from within the BUF (probably P.G. Taylor) stressed the revolutionary rhetoric of in-

---

[20] PRO: CAB 15/7, WM 128(40), p. 177.

ternal meetings with the Fascists leading the defence against the supposed threat of a Communist revolution during the war.

Taylor also heard through Aubrey Lees of meetings in the autumn of 1939 which showed that the various elements of the Fascist fringe of British politics were trying to co-operate with one another. Mosley had a series of meetings with Archibald H. Maule Ramsay MP, Sir Barry Domvile and other members of the Nordic League, the Link and Information and Policy. Domvile was also connected with the British Council for Christian Settlement in Europe which was dominated by the British People's party.[21] During the autumn of 1939 these 'secret meetings' were viewed dispassionately by MI5. According to Domvile's diary they appear to have been about the threat of internment, mutual collaboration and setting up a newspaper advocating peace. When the security situation deteriorated after March 1940 such continued gatherings were portrayed in rather more sinister light by the authorities. Sir John Anderson later reported that although there was no evidence which could justify the prosecution of Fascists there had been reason to believe that they were preparing secret plans which would enable them, in the event of an invasion of this country, either to range themselves on the side of the enemy, or by a *coup d'état* to seize power and make terms with them.[22] As there was no evidence of secretive subversive activity by the Communists they were warned as to their future behaviour by having the *Daily Worker* and the *Week* closed down. It has recently been suggested that MI5 were worried about possible Fascist contact with William Joyce in Germany and the activities of the New British Broadcasting Service.[23] Internment of Fascists was seen partly as a way of stopping such connections.

Whilst one group of agents was establishing closer connection between the Fascists (Taylor, Kurtz *et al.*), another group had infiltrated the Right Club and discovered a real breach of national security. The Tyler Kent affair showed that the Germans, via the Italian embassy in London, were possibly receiving some information about the secret correspondence between President Franklin D. Roosevelt and Winston Churchill, through the passing on of material by the cypher clerk, Kent, to Anna Wolkoff, the political secretary of Archibald Ramsay MP, who had also been shown several top secret documents. Also Wolkoff was alleged by MI5 to have passed on to the Germans top secret information about the Narvik raid. The tenuous connection between Mosley and Ramsay was seen as sufficient to intern

[21] Domvile papers, Dom 56, diary 1939–40.
[22] PRO: CAB 98/18.
[23] *Comrade* No 11, March 1988.

BUF members as well as the Right Club and other fringe groups.[24]

The suspicions voiced against British Fascists have to be seen in the light of fears about security leaks from within the British Establishment. The security authorities were worried about possible leaks from those who had contact with the war cabinet and supreme war council. German Foreign Office documents suggest that the Duke of Windsor was sometimes less than discreet in discussing operations and General Ironside's diary for 1940 mentions both security leaks and the 'whispering campaign' against him personally.[25] On 28 May Vernon Kell, the Director-General of MI5, was sacked and national security was overseen by the Swinton Committee, the Home Defence (Security Executive). The collapse of western Europe before the nazi *blitzkrieg* in the spring of 1940 was the essential backcloth to the security revolution. Whether the Fascists, and even more innocent aliens, were made the scapegoat for increased security consciousness is not clear. We know very little about the security aspects of Ultra intercepts although this seems to have been one of the sources of MI5 fears about Tyler Kent. However even given this the internment of 747 Fascists under defence regulation 18b appears to have been an over-reaction, as was the banning of British Union in July 1940.

Thus the failure of British fascism represented a mixture of its own inadequacies, the apathy or hostility of sections of British society, and government action. The means of its demise was to have permanent effect on many who were interned. Above all the shock to an organisation which had prided itself on being ultra-patriotic being accused, without evidence, of being potential traitors was a physical and psychological scar many failed to recover from. Others were to become even more dedicated Mosleyites under the auspices of the Union Movement. Yet whatever the reactions to internment it must be remembered that the cause of fascism's failure has to be seen elsewhere. Internment was merely a sledgehammer to crack a nut. The weaknesses of British fascism had long been apparent, a veritable catalogue of negative characteristics which ensured that it could never be of more than marginal significance to the politics of the inter-war years.

---

[24] PRO: CAB 65/13, WM 133 (40), 22 May 1940; W.J. West, *Truth Betrayed* (1987), pp. 201–44.

[25] *Documents on German Foreign Policy 1918–45* Series D, vol. VIII, 4 Sept. 1939 to 18 March 1940, p. 785; R. McCleod and D. Kelly (eds.), *The Ironside Diaries 1937–40* (1962), pp. 93, 384.

Further Reading

Labour and the Frustration of the Extreme Left

The most detailed, and still in many ways the best book on the inter-war Labour party remains G.D.H. Cole, *A History of the Labour Party From 1914* (1948). C.F. Brand, *The British Labour Party* (1965) and the shorter but often incisive H. Pelling, *A Short History of the Labour Party* (6th. edn., 1978) are good alternatives. R. Miliband, *Parliamentary Socialism* (2nd. edn., 1972), and D. Coates, *The Labour Party and the Struggle for Socialism* (1975), are both more critical, arguing that Labour should have taken a less parliament-oriented line. The ILP is well covered in R.E. Dowse, *Left in the Centre* (1966). R.I. McKibbin, *The Evolution of the Labour Party* (Oxford, 1974) is interesting on early relations with the Communists, while B. Pimlott, *Labour and the Left in the 1930s* does the same, and much else, for the later period and shows just how pale the red of that controversial decade really was. J. Jupp, *The Radical Left in Britain, 1931–1941* (1982) is an admirably clear account of a highly complex subject; it is especially revealing on relations between the ILP and the CPGB. Three contemporary foreign views of Labour offer a fascinating variety of interpretations: L.D. Trotsky, *Where Is Britain Going?* (1926), E. Wertheimer, *Portrait of the Labour Party* (1929), and D.E. McHenry, *The Labour Party in Transition, 1931–1938* (1938).

On the unions, the standard work is H.A. Clegg, *A History of British Trade Unions since 1889, vol. 2: 1911–1933* (Oxford, 1985), although there are excellent analytical essays by Patrick Renshaw and Richard Shackleton in B. Pimlott and C. Cook (eds.), *Trade Unions in British Politics* (1982).

Of the major leaders discussed, a number are well-served by biographers: D. Marquand, *Ramsay MacDonald* (1977); K. Harris, *Attlee* (1982); B. Pimlott, *Hugh Dalton* (1985); B. Donoughue and G.W. Jones, *Herbert Morrison* (1973); A. Bullock, *The Life and Times of Ernest Bevin* (3 vols., 1960–85). Cripps, Snowden, Thomas, Clynes (unsurprisingly) and Henderson all lack good modern lives, although in the last case the defect can be remedied somewhat, pending the publication of a short biography by C.J. Wrigley, by reference to R.I. McKibbin, 'Arthur Henderson as Labour leader', *International Review of Social History*, 23 (1978), and A.J. Thorpe, 'Arthur Henderson and the British political crisis of 1931', *Historical Journal*, 31, 1 (1988).

The ideological aspect is covered in G. Foote, *The Labour Party's Political Thought* (1985), although the works by Durbin, MacDonald and Henderson cited in the footnotes merit consultation in their own right.

The broader aspects of working-class attitudes and activities, and their political implications, can be followed in P. Johnson, *Saving and Spending: the working-class economy in Britain, 1870–1939* (Oxford, 1985); S. Macintyre, 'British Labour, Marxism and working-class apathy in the 1920s', *Historical Journal*, 20, 2 (1977); and two articles by R.I. McKibbin, 'Why was there no Marxism in Great Britain?, *English Historical Review*, 99, 2 (1984), and 'Work and hobbies in Britain, 1880–1950', in J.M. Winter (ed.), *The Working Class in Modern British History* (1983).

Finally, new light is shed on Labour's behaviour and working-class political responses in Britain's most serious inter-war political crisis in A.J. Thorpe, 'The British general election of 1931', University of Sheffield Ph.D. thesis, 1987.

The Failure of the Communists

W. Hannington's books on unemployment and on his experiences as NUWM national organiser, *Unemployed Struggles 1919–1936* (1936), *The Problem of the Distressed Areas* (1937) and *Ten Lean Years* (1940) are — together with his autobiography, *Never on Our Knees* (1967) — essential reading but his wilder claims need to be taken with a pinch of salt. H. McShane and J. Smith, *Harry McShane No Mean Fighter* (1977), the memoirs of an ex-Communist willing to discuss party failings, contain much valuable detail and insight. P. Kingsford, *The Hunger Marchers in Britain, 1920–1940* (1982) is a useful narrative which, however, often fails to question Hannington's assertions. R. Croucher, *We Refuse to Starve in Silence* (1987) broadens discussion on the NUWM as an organisation. H.J.P. Harmer, 'The National Unemployed Workers' Movement in Britain, 1921–1939: Failure and Success', University of London (LSE) Ph.D. thesis, 1987 examines Communist strategy and tactics, concentrating on the distance between what the unemployed who joined the NUWM wanted from it and what the party expected of them. W. Brierley's novel *Means Test Man* (1935, reprinted Nottingham, 1983) gives sympathetic insight into the individual tragedy of unemployment and the lack of political confidence almost invariably engendered.

There are a number of works on the Communist party itself. J. Klugmann, *History of the Communist Party of Great Britain* (2 vols., 1976), the official history up to 1926, makes dull reading but needs to be referred to. N. Branson, *History of the Communist Party of Great Britain, 1927–1941* (1985) is more vividly written and, for the most part, honestly confronts a difficult period in Communist history. L.J. McFarlane, *The British Communist Party: its origin and development until 1929* (1966) remains useful, and S. Macintyre's examination of local activity in *Little Moscows: Communism and working-class militancy in inter-war Britain* (1980) makes many valuable points about a party which often had a greater local than national impact. In this context, the personal memoirs of E. Trory, *Between the Wars: recollections of a Communist organiser* (Brighton, 1974), B. Darke, *The Communist Technique in Britain* (1953) and J. Jacobs, *Out of the Ghetto* (1978) are worth reading, acknowledging an element of bitterness in the latter two books. R. Martin, *Communism and British Trade Unions, 1924–1933: a study of the National Minority Movement* (Oxford, 1969), examines the relationship between communism and the unions and provides a parallel with the NUWM. For the documentary background to pressures from the Comintern, and for a revelation of how out of touch Moscow usually was, J. Degras, *The Communist International, 1919–1943: Documents* (3 vols., Oxford, 1956–65) might almost be — if the results for Europe were not so tragic — amusing reading.

The Conservatives and the Frustration of the Extreme Right

Outline coverage of the Conservative party in this period is provided, with something of a 'house' flavour, by R. Blake, *The Conservative Party from Peel to Churchill* (1970), and T. Lindsay and M. Harrington, *The Conservative Party 1918–1979* (1979), although the best textbook treatment so far is J. Ramsden, *The Age of Balfour and Baldwin, 1902–1940* (1978). Useful essays can be found, by J.H. Grainger and the editor, in D. Southgate (ed.), *The Conservative Leadership 1832–1932* (1974), and by D. Dilks in Lord

Butler (ed.), *The Conservatives* (1977). Among the better biographies of the successive party leaders are R. Blake, *The Unknown Prime Minister: the life and times of Andrew Bonar Law* (1955); R.K. Middlemas and J. Barnes, *Baldwin* (1969) and H.M. Hyde, *Baldwin* (1973); K. Feiling, *The Life of Neville Chamberlain* (1946), and D. Dilks, *Neville Chamberlain, vol. 1* (1984), which goes up to 1929; and on Churchill the monumental biographical series completed by M. Gilbert, particularly *vol. V, 1922–1939* (1976), and R. Rhodes James, *Churchill: a study in failure, 1900–1939* (1970). Also worth attention are A.J.P. Taylor, *Beaverbrook* (1972), and the papers of J.C.C. Davidson, Baldwin's sometime party chairman, edited by R. Rhodes James as *Memoirs of a Conservative* (1969).

For the opening years of the period, see K.O. Morgan *Consensus and Disunity* (Oxford, 1979); J. Stubbs, 'The impact of the Great War on the Conservative party', in G. Peele and C. Cook (eds.), *The Politics of Reappraisal, 1918–1939* (1975); W.D. Rubinstein, 'Henry Page Croft and the National party, 1918– 22', *Journal of Contemporary History*, 9 (1974); D. Close, 'Conservatives and Coalition after the First World War', *Journal of Modern History*, 45 (1973); and M. Cowling, *The Impact of Labour, 1920–1924* (Cambridge, 1975). The last theme is extended beyond the Labour party to the unions by P. Renshaw in 'Anti-Labour politics in Britain 1918–27', *Journal of Contemporary History*, 12 (1977), and in his *The General Strike* (1975). For the end and aftermath of Baldwin's second ministry there are P. Williamson, 'Safety First: Baldwin, the Conservative party, and the 1929 general election', *Historical Journal*, 25 (1982), and S. Ball, *Baldwin and the Conservative Party: the crisis of 1929–1931* (1988), the fullest study of that phase, though G. Peele, 'St George's and the Empire Crusade', in C. Cook and J. Ramsden (eds.), *By-Elections in British Politics* (1973) remains valuable. Though there is no monograph on the Tory response to the formation and course of the National government, T. Stannage, *Baldwin Thwarts the Opposition* (1980), covers the 1935 general election.

G.C. Webber, *The Ideology of the British Right, 1918–1939* (1986), seeks to identify and analyse a 'right' partly within and partly outside the Conservative party. J.R. Jones's essay 'England' in H. Rogger and E. Weber (eds.), *The European Right* (1965), still repays attention. For the Indian question see G. Peele, 'The Revolt over India', in *The Politics of Reappraisal*, and S.C. Ghosh, 'Decision-making in the British Conservative party: a case study of the Indian problem, 1929–34', *Political Studies*, 13 (1965). For the impact of European fascism on the British right see R. Bosworth, 'The British press, the Conservatives and Mussolini, 1920–34', *Journal of Contemporary History*, 5 (1970); F.R. Gannon, *The British*

Press and Germany, 1936-1939 (Oxford, 1971); M. Cowling, *The Impact of Hitler* (Cambridge, 1975); R. Griffiths, *Fellow Travellers of the Right: British enthusiasts for Nazi Germany, 1933-39* (1980); and N. Thompson, *The Anti-Appeasers: Conservative opposition to appeasement in the 1930s* (Oxford, 1971).

B. Harrison, 'The centrist theme in modern British politics', in his *Peaceable Kingdom: stability and change in modern Britain* (Oxford, 1982) is stimulating, not only for the present topic. The unevenness of the economic and political experience of inter-war Britain can be gauged from J. Stevenson and C. Cook, *The Slump* (1977), while electoral patterns can be studied in M. Kinnear, *The British Voter* (Ithica, NY, 1968), and in F.W.S. Craig (ed.), *British Parliamentary Election Results, 1918-1949* (Glasgow, 1969), and *Minor Parties at British Parliamentary Elections, 1885-1974* (1975).

The Failure of the Fascists

The recent publication of R. Thurlow, *Fascism in Britain: a history, 1918-1985* (Oxford, 1987), D.S. Lewis, *Illusions of Grandeur* (Manchester, 1987), and G. Webber, *The British Right* (1986) represent the beginning of renewed interest in the growth industry of the study of British fascism which will be further stimulated by the publication of K. Lunn and A. Kushner (eds.), *Traditions of Intolerance* (Manchester, 1989). Indeed new material from Fascist, anti-Fascist and intelligence sources is becoming available and it will be interesting to see how forthcoming studies by S. Cullen and J. Hope lead in revolutionary new directions. Of older works R. Skidelsky, *Oswald Mosley* (1975), N. Mosley, *Rules of the game* (1981) and *Beyond the Pale* (1983) present interesting views of the controversial personality of Sir Oswald Mosley. C. Cross, *The Fascists in Britain* (1961) is a good introduction to the subject despite some factual inaccuracies. R. Benewick, *The Fascist Movement in Britain* (1972) is still useful for the study of political violence. G. Anderson, *Fascists, Communists and the National Government* (1983) is useful for state management of British fascism but new material has become available in the HO 45, HO 144 and HO 283 files at the Public Record Office since it was written. On anti-semitism and British fascism readers should consult G. Lebzelter, *Political Anti-Semitism in England, 1918-1939* (1979), C. Holmes, *Anti-Semitism in British Society, 1876-1939* (1979), and W. Mandle, *Anti-Semitism and the British Union of Fascists* (1965). On right-wing and Fascist attitudes towards Germany and Italy see R. Griffiths, *Fellow Travellers of the Right* (1980). On the sociology of British fascism see J. Brewer, *Mosley's Men* (1984) and

G. Webber, 'Patterns of membership and support for the British Union of Fascists', *Journal of Contemporary History*, 19 (1984). A useful cross-section of research on British fascism is to be found in K. Lunn and R. Thurlow (eds.), *British Fascism* (1980). There are several good unpublished theses on various aspects of British fascism before 1939 of which the most interesting the author has read are D. Baker, 'A.K. Chesterton: the making of a British Fascist', University of Sheffield Ph.D. thesis, 1982, and S. Rawnsley, 'Fascism and Fascists in Britain in the 1930s', University of Bradford Ph.D. thesis, 1983.

Notes on Contributors

Bruce Coleman is a Senior Lecturer in the Department of History and Archaeology, University of Exeter. His *Conservatism and the Conservative Party in Nineteenth-Century Britain* was published by Edward Arnold in 1988.

Harry Harmer took a History degree at the Polytechnic of North London after working in a wide variety of jobs. He went on to research at the LSE. He now works in a library in London, is writing a book on the National Unemployed Workers' Movement, and has three children, Anna, Tom and Rosie.

Andrew Thorpe is a Lecturer in the Department of History and Archaeology, University of Exeter. He has just completed *The British General Election of 1931* and is about to embark on a full-scale biography of Arthur Henderson.

Richard Thurlow is a Lecturer in the Department of History, University of Sheffield. He is author of *Fascism in Britain 1918-85* (Basil Blackwell, 1987) and is currently working on political extremism and internal security in twentieth-century Britain.

EXETER STUDIES IN HISTORY

Publications

No. 1   *The Military Revolution and the State 1500–1800*
edited by Michael Duffy

No. 2   *Government, Party and People in Nazi Germany*
edited by Jeremy Noakes

No. 3   *'Into Another Mould': Aspects of the Interregnum*
edited by Ivan Roots

No. 4   *Problems and Case Studies in Archaeological Dating*
edited by Bryony Orme

No. 5   *Britain and Revolutionary France: Conflict, Subversion and Propaganda*
edited by Colin Jones

No. 6   *Nazism 1919–1945 A Documentary Reader 1: The Rise to Power 1919–1934*
edited by J. Noakes and G. Pridham

No. 7   *Roman Political Life 90BC–AD69*
edited by T. P. Wiseman

No. 8   *Nazism 1919–1945 A Documentary Reader 2:*
State, Economy and Society 1933–39
edited by J. Noakes and G. Pridham

No. 9   *Africa, America and Central Asia:*
Formal and Informal Empire in the Nineteenth Century
edited by Peter Morris

No. 10   *'Raleigh in Exeter': Privateering and Colonisation in the Reign of Elizabeth I*
edited by Joyce Youings

No. 11   *The First Portuguese Colonial Empire*
edited by Malyn Newitt

No. 12   *The Inheritance of Historiography, 350–900*
edited by Christopher Holdsworth and T. P. Wiseman

No. 13   *Nazism 1919–1945 A Documentary Reader 3:*
Foreign Policy, War and Racial Extermination
edited by J. Noakes and G. Pridham

No. 14   *Domesday Essays*
edited by Christopher Holdsworth

No. 15   *Intelligence and International Relations 1900–1945*
edited by Christopher Andrew and Jeremy Noakes

No. 16   *The American Constitution. The First Two Hundred Years 1787–1987*
edited by Joseph Smith

No. 17   *The Compromising of Louis XVI:*
The Armoire de Fer and the French Revolution
by Andrew Freeman

No. 18   *The Administration of the Roman Empire*
edited by David Braund

No. 19   *Security and Defence in South-West England before 1800*
edited by Robert Higham

No. 20   *Roman Public Buildings*
edited by I. M. Barton